The 500 Hidden Secrets of
PARIS

INTRODUCTION

This guide invites you to leave the beaten track and explore unknown and surprising places in Paris. As you leaf through the guide and examine the categories you will discover intimate restaurants, unusual stores, secret passages as well as the favourite haunts of the Parisians themselves. Among others this guide lists the 5 best cooking courses in Paris, the 5 most charming small museums and 5 unusual places where you can have a really fun evening.

The main objective of this publication is to guide the reader to the places that are not usually included in tourist guides. Like the most beautiful artists' studios or an Italian restaurant with only six tables or even a magnificent view of Paris from the rooftop of a department store. At the same time it also lists small jewellery designers, splendid stationery shops and many other places, cafes, galleries, and stores that are bound to knock your socks off.

This guide also includes some unusual experiences, like hopping on a bus because it allows you to see all the most beautiful monuments in Paris, a picnic in a secret garden in the heart of the historic Marais neighbourhood or taking your children to a fantastic costume shop. You can also explore unexpected details in Paris like old billboards from the Fifties, which you would have never noticed otherwise.

Finally this guide does not mention everything you can see and do in Paris. Many a guide has already been written on this subject. The aim of this guide is to be intimate, personal, based on experience and surprising. The author shares her favourite places with her readers, much as she would do with a friend interested in visiting Paris, the most loved city in Europe.

HOW TO USE
THIS GUIDE

———

This guide lists 500 places to go in Paris. There are 100 different categories, with five places each. Most of these are places to visit. We have included practical information like the address, the phone number or the website. For certain events we have also listed the opening hours. The purpose of this guide is to inspire you to explore the city but it does not cover every aspect, from A to Z.

We have also added map details that will help you locate these places. The number of the arrondissement is indicated, in view of the fact that the centre of Paris is subdivided into 20 *arrondissements* or districts that form a spiral, like a snail shell, fanning out clockwise from the city centre to the périphérique or ring road. In this guide the letter A is followed by the number of the arrondissement.

What's more, we have also indicated the neighbourhood where each place is, for example Quartier Latin or Marais. The code 'LB' or 'RB' (that indicates whether the place is on the left or right bank of the Seine) is followed by the number of the map to which it refers. The maps can be found in the beginning of the guide.

Each place is numbered from 1 to 500. This number helps you locate it on the maps. A word of caution however: these maps are not detailed enough to allow you to locate specific locations in the city. You can obtain an excellent map from any tourist office or in most hotels.

The author also wishes to emphasise that a city like Paris constantly changes. So a delicious meal at a restaurant may not be quite as good on the day you visit it. This personal and subjective selection is based on the author's experience, at the time that this guide was compiled. If you want to add a comment, suggest a correction, recommend a place or share your own secret place in Paris with us then contact the editor at info@lusterweb.com.

THE AUTHOR

Marie Farman is a true Parisian. She was born in Paris and lives in the city with her partner and their son. According to Marie every neighbourhood has its treasures, whether a small courtyard hidden behind a doorway, a quiet street in the urban jungle or a small square lined with cafés. Her advice? Look up to see the subtle details, like the balconies and the flowers or the splendid stained glass windows. Sit in sidewalk cafés to witness scenes of life in the city. Stroll around aimlessly and be surprised by the unparalleled beauty of a city whose vibrant spirit continues to inspire this Parisian and make her dream.

As a design journalist Marie's job takes her across Paris daily as she enthusiastically discovers different facets of city life, during interviews, exhibitions and visits of design studios.

The author wishes to thank the many people who helped her gather these 500 places. Her family, her friends, friends of friends, colleagues, her neighbours or even strangers during chance encounters. Without their precious help it would have been impossible to draw up a list of so many places, some of which are unknown to tourists but which any self-respecting Parisian cannot live out and others that embody the spirit of Paris.

PARIS

overview

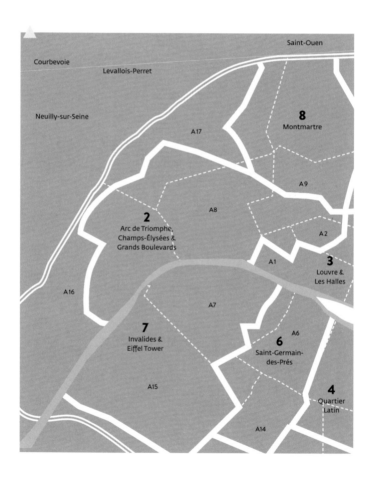

Saint-Ouen

Courbevoie

Levallois-Perret

Neuilly-sur-Seine

A17

8
Montmartre

A9

2
Arc de Triomphe,
Champs-Élysées &
Grands Boulevards

A8

A2

A1

3
Louvre &
Les Halles

A16

A7

7
Invalides &
Eiffel Tower

A6

6
Saint-Germain-
des-Prés

4
Quartier
Latin

A15

A14

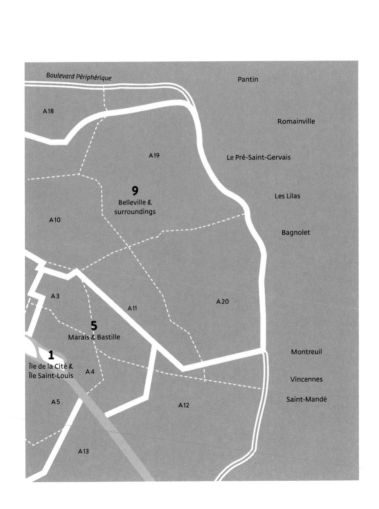

Boulevard Périphérique

Pantin

A18

Romainville

A19

Le Pré-Saint-Gervais

9
Belleville &
surroundings

Les Lilas

A10

Bagnolet

A3

A11

A20

5
Marais & Bastille

1
Île de la Cité &
Île Saint-Louis

A4

Montreuil

Vincennes

A5

A12

Saint-Mandé

A13

Map 1
ÎLE DE LA CITÉ &
ÎLE SAINT-LOUIS

Map 2
ARC DE TRIOMPHE,
CHAMPS-ÉLYSÉES &
GRANDS BOULEVARDS (RB)

Map 3
LOUVRE & LES HALLES
(RB)

Map 4
QUARTIER LATIN
(L B)

Map 5
MARAIS & BASTILLE (RB)

Map 6
SAINT-GERMAIN-DES-PRÉS
& MONTPARNASSE (LB)

Map 7
INVALIDES &
EIFFEL TOWER (LB)

Map 8
MONTMARTRE (RB)

Map 9
BELLEVILLE &
SURROUNDINGS (RB)

CHEZ JEANNETTE

120 PLACES TO EAT OR BUY GOOD FOOD

The 5 best
TRADITIONAL BISTROS
in Paris

1 **AU PETIT FER À CHEVAL**

30 rue Vieille du Temple
A4 - Marais & Bastille
(RB) ⑤
+33 (0)1 42 72 47 47
*www.cafeine.com/
petit-fer-a-cheval*

With its horse-shoe shaped zinc bar and the dining room behind it, its mosaic floor and tiny terrace this genuine Paris bistro is a must visit in the Marais. The menu features several staples of traditional French cuisine, including some memorable desserts like *tarte tatin*. Patrons have been known to strike up a conversation or a long-standing friendship with the people at the neighbouring table the time of a drink or a meal.

2 **LE PETIT MARCEL**

65 rue Rambuteau
A3 - Louvre &
Les Halles (RB) ③
+33 (0)1 48 87 10 20

This Paris bistro, which is located between les Halles and Centre Pompidou, opened at the end of the 19th century. Its charming and typically Parisian interior as well as the menu which includes several traditional French dishes have attracted a heterogeneous clientele of locals and tourists. They gather around the beautiful wood bar to share their latest news.

3 **LE BAR DU MARCHÉ**

75 rue de Seine
A6 - Saint-Germain-des-Prés & Mont-parnasse (LB) ⑥
+33 (0)1 43 26 55 15

The bar's perfect location on the corner of rue de Seine and rue de Buci, in the heart of Saint-Germain-des-Prés, have made it a great local institution. Although it is sometimes difficult to find a table on the terrace, winter and summer alike, once you do score one your patience will be rewarded by the excellent people watching in this bustling neighbourhood.

4 LA PALETTE

43 rue de Seine
A6 - Saint-Germain-
des-Prés & Mont-
parnasse (LB) ⑥
+33 (0)1 43 26 68 15
*www.cafelapaletteparis.
com*

The façade of this iconic bistro is listed as a historical monument. La Palette is simply timeless because of its infamous terrace which gives out onto rue Jacques-Callot, a narrow pedestrian street. Students from the nearby art schools can be found here at all times of the day as well as the owners of the art galleries in the neighbourhood, who claim this bar as their headquarters.

5 LE PURE CAFÉ

14 rue Jean Mace
A11 - Marais & Bastille
(RB) ⑤
+33 (0)1 83 76 03 33
www.purecafe.fr

This is the archetypal Parisian bistro, with its magnificent façade, its wood and zinc bar, tiles on the floor and mirrors on the wall. The new owners have skilfully updated the interior while maintaining the authentic elements of this neighbourhood haunt, which is popular with people of all ages.

4 LA PALETTE

5 good
BRASSERIES

---

6   **LE CHARDENOUX**
1 rue Jules Vallès
A11 - Marais & Bastille
(RB) ⑤
+33 (0)1 43 71 49 52
*www.restaurant
lechardenoux.com*

First opened in Paris in 1908 this is one of the last true Parisian bistros in existence and a real historical monument. Large mirrors hang on the walls and the original marble mosaic bar and floor tiles are still in place. As a result Le Chardenoux has managed to retain its old world elegance and pleasant atmosphere. A few years ago the French chef Cyril Lignac took over at the helm of the kitchen, giving pride of place to French cuisine and regional products, revisiting traditional dishes and reinterpreting them with a modern twist. A delightful experience.

7   **LE BISTROT VIVIENNE**
4 rue des Petits Champs
A2 – Louvre & Les Halles (RB) ③
+33 (0)1 49 27 00 50
www.bistrotvivienne.com

Location, location, location… This brasserie, which is located at the entrance of Galerie Vivienne, a covered passage which was built in 1823, has taken advantage of this to set up a few tables in this stunning covered arcade. But the dining room inside is also a nice place to enjoy a good meal, because this Paris bistro is known for its delicious traditional bistro cuisine.

7 LE BISTROT VIVIENNE

9 LE RICHER

www. bistrotpeintre .com
Bistrot du Peintre (duck)
116 avre-rue Ledru-Rollin

8 BISTROT PAUL BERT

18 rue Paul Bert
A11 - Marais & Bastille
(RB) ⑤
+33 (0)1 43 72 24 01

Step into this bistro and it's like stepping into a postcard, without all the clichés however. The clientele consists of a nice blend of tourists and locals, largely because this place serves exactly what they expect: reassuringly good food, which has been cooked as they should be, like a nice steak béarnaise with hand-cut French fries or an old-style *crème caramel*, combined with an upbeat atmosphere and impeccable service.

9 LE RICHER

2 rue Richer
A9 - Montmartre (RB)
⑧

This place is the incarnation of the new Parisian 'bistronomy'. Against a backdrop of exposed brick walls, the emphasis is on what's on your plate which is served to you by an attentive waiter. The menu is minimal at best but it gives pride of place to seasonal products, which have been prepared with a creative twist and a light-handed approach. We recommend arriving early for lunch and dinner because they do not accept reservations and Le Richer is such a hit that it is often difficult to find a table here during peak times.

10 LE BARATIN

3 rue Jouye-Rouve
A20 - Belleville &
surroundings (RB) ⑨
+33 (0)1 43 49 39 70

This bistro is tucked away in a discreet street in the working-class Belleville neighbourhood and comes highly recommended. Because the interior decoration is random at best and the welcome is not always as warm as you might expect people often wonder what all the fuss is about. But wait until you've tasted their food! Chef Raquel Carena puts her heart and all her expertise in the dishes she serves! She handpicks her products, specialising in divine combinations and a nice presentation.

Saveurs & Coincidences - 6 rue de Trévise

5 restaurants for a
ROMANTIC DINNER

11 **MAISON DE L'AMÉRIQUE LATINE**

217 boulevard Saint-Germain
A7 - Invalides & Eiffel Tower (LB) ⑦
+33 (0)1 49 54 75 10
mal217.org

A chic yet discreet place to have an intimate lunch or dinner. As soon as the sun comes out, from May to September, the tables are set on the terrace which overlooks a magnificent French garden. The elegant and pastoral setting will immediately make you forget the noise and traffic of boulevard Saint-Germain from which you enter this 18th-century mansion. Chef Thierry Vaissière serves colourful, refined and light food.

12 **LE 404**

69 rue des Gravilliers
A3 - Marais & Bastille (RB) ⑤
+33 (0)1 42 74 57 81
www.404-resto.com

This Moroccan restaurant is the perfect place for a romantic dinner. In spite of the proximity of the tables the atmosphere is lively, welcoming and exotic, thanks to the elaborate interior design with its muted light and the mashrabiyas. It's as if you're having dinner in Morocco, not Paris! The traditional dishes, like chicken and pear tajine or milk bastillas also take you on a voyage of discovery.

13 LE SERGENT RECRUTEUR

41 rue Saint-Louis en l'Isle

A4 - Île de la Cité & Île Saint-Louis ①

+33 (0)1 43 54 75 42

www.lesergentrecruteur.fr

This intimate restaurant in the very romantic Île Saint-Louis is the place that immediately comes to mind for a romantic dinner. Chef Antonin Bonnet joined forces with designer Jamie Hayon for this Michelin-starred restaurant. Whether you decide to go for the 'carte blanche' menu, following the chef's whims in the dining room or enjoy a refined snack at the bar instead you will never be disappointed by the elaborate dishes prepared with seasonal, simple products, sourced from France for the most part and which are subtly transformed into something absolutely exquisite.

14 CHEZ JULIEN

1 rue du Pont Louis-Philippe

A4 – Marais & Bastille (RB) ⑤

+33 (0)1 42 78 31 64

www.beaumarly.com/chez-julien/accueil

This place is a combination of all the clichés of a romantic restaurant: its location between the Marais and Île Saint-Louis, its belle époque interior with wood panels and mirrors, its plush ambiance, its menu with traditional dishes and its magnificent terrace with a view of nearby Eglise Saint-Gervais. But it has to be said that although it does almost resemble a film set this restaurant is quite magical.

15 VERJUS

52 rue de Richelieu

A1 - Louvre & Les Halles (RB) ③

+33 (0)1 42 97 54 40

verjusparis.com

You walk through the tiny passage de Beaujolais, near the gates to the Palais-Royal to get to Verjus. This exceptional location is already a harbinger of the poetic evening that awaits you. This exquisite bistro, which was acquired by an American team, serves a seven-course tasting menu, which gives pride of place to seasonal vegetables and typical French products.

5 *restaurants*
where you can enjoy
AUTHENTIC CUISINE

---

16 SEPTIME

80 rue de Charonne
A11 – Marais & Bastille
(RB) ⑤
+33 (0)1 43 67 38 29
www.septime-charonne.fr

Here the interior and the food you are served are consistent with each other as they are both poetic and visually pleasing. The chef of Septime, Grégoire Thiebault, is one of the new generation of young Parisian restaurant owners. They honour the French terroir and take a pure and spontaneous approach to its products. The friendly and discreet welcome adds a nice finishing touch to this incomparable restaurant which never seems to have a table available. So much so that you sometimes have to wait several weeks before you have the good fortune to dine here.

17 LE CLOWN BAR

114 rue Amelot
A11 – Marais & Bastille
(RB) ⑤
+33 (0)1 43 55 87 35

This little neighbourhood bistro right next to the winter circus has been around for ages but has recently been revived thanks to a young team who knows what they're doing. We love the small appetizers that you can munch on at the bar or share with friends around one of the tables on the terrace – a bit like a sophisticated kind of tapas. And then there's the dessert menu and the friendly staff: two more reasons to choose this bar as one of your favourite Paris hangouts.

18 LE GALOPIN

34 rue Sainte-Marthe
A10 – Belleville &
surroundings (RB) ⑨
+33 (0)1 42 06 05 03
www.le-galopin.com

The Tischenko brothers serve lunch and dinner in their gastronomic bistro with a simple interior design which gives out onto pretty place Sainte-Marthe. Romain is the chef and he believes in a minimal and intuitive approach to cuisine. Of course all the produce is meticulously sourced and the wines for the most part are natural wines.

19 FRENCHIE

5-6 rue du Nil
A2 – Louvre &
Les Halles (RB) ③
+33 (0)1 40 39 96 19
www.frenchie-restaurant.com

Grégory Marchand is the figurehead of a new generation of chefs who have overturned the precepts of French cuisine. The restaurant is such a hit that you have to reserve a table weeks and sometimes months in advance. But his eatery on narrow rue pavée du Sentier can only seat 20, which partly explains why it is so difficult to get in. The menu includes a lot of seasonal dishes, inspired by traditional French cuisine and transformed by his international experiences.

20 BONES

43 rue Godefroy
Cavaignac
A11 – Marais & Bastille
(RB) ⑤
+33 (0)9 80 75 32 08
www.bonesparis.com

A bare bones wall, a busy ambiance, bistro tables… You may not think so at first but Bones is one of the most popular restaurants of the moment. Everyone is talking about the young Australian chef James Henry and gourmets all over the city are waxing eloquently about his inspired, bold and spontaneous cuisine. If you like discoveries then Bones, with its 'menu fixe' that tends towards the experimental, is just the place for you.

The 5 best
VEGETARIAN OR
ORGANIC *restaurants*

---

21 **BOB'S KITCHEN**

74 rue des Gravilliers
A3 – Marais & Bastille
(RB) ⑤
+33 (0)9 52 55 11 66
www.bobsjuicebar.com

In just a few years the American Marc Grossmann, an organic food guru, has succeeded in revolutionising 'healthy' restaurant food in Paris. His juice bar, his two vegetarian canteens and his bakery are the hotspot for anyone who loves seeds and grains, vegetables and fruit juices that will energise you. The atmosphere of these laidback restaurants is cool and hip.

22 **SUPERNATURE**

15 rue de Trévise
A9 – Louvre &
Les Halles (RB) ③
+33 (0)1 42 46 58 04
www.super-nature.fr

This restaurant not only looks nice – think clear lines, lots of white and natural materials – but also has a great lunch and dinner menu featuring sophisticated dishes made with lots of seasonal vegetables. There's a second Supernature restaurant a little further down the street, and also a takeaway.

23 CAFÉ PINSON

6 rue du Forez
A3 – Marais & Bastille
(RB) ⑤
+33 (0)9 83 82 53 53
www.cafepinson.fr

Your eye will be first drawn to the lovely interior design by decorator Dorothée Meilichzon. Then, after you have checked out the menu, you will realise that this is definitely a haven for those who enjoy vegetarian and whole foods: gluten-free, meat-free, dairy-free… in fact the kitchen believes in a no-dairy approach. And yet many a customer enjoys the tasty fare that is served here, including the chocolate, which although it is made without butter, tastes just as good, if not better.

24 SOYA

20 rue de la Pierre
Levée
A11 – Belleville &
surroundings (RB) ⑨
+33 (0)1 48 06 33 02

This organic canteen was one of the first in its kind in Paris. Tucked away in a tiny street near Canal Saint-Martin Soya was also one of the first organic eateries with a more modern, airy interior, combining industrial architecture with large wooden tables on which copious and appetizing dishes are served. The place has been popular since it opened, largely thanks to the delicious vegetarian couscous on the menu.

25 GUENMAI

6 rue Cardinale
A6 – Saint-Germain-
des-Prés & Mont-
parnasse (LB) ⑥
+33 (0)1 43 26 03 24

This greengrocer's/restaurant in Saint-Germain-des-Prés is popular with fans of seitan, tofu or soy milk. Here organic is not just another flash marketing word but a real philosophy as you can tell by the large sign on the window: *la santé par l'alimentation* (achieving health through food). Fortunately this place looks nothing like a doctor's office. In fact you might even say there is something charming about the wicker chairs and the tiny terrace. The food is colourful and tasty.

The 5 best
EXOTIC RESTAURANTS

---

26 BERNICA

4 impasse de la Gaité
A 14 – Saint-Germain-
des-Prés & Mont-
parnasse (LB) ⑥
+33 (0)1 43 20 39 02
*www.restaurant-
reunionnais-paris.fr*

At Bernica you can discover the signature dishes of Réunion, that stunning French gem of the Indian Ocean. One very popular dish, which is typical of the island's exotic Creole cuisine, is the infamous rougail morue or cod rougail and the sweet potato cake. The warm welcome of the owners who have had this restaurant for over 30 years, also adds an exotic touch.

27 LOUBNANE

29 rue Galande
A 5 – Quartier Latin
(LB) ④
+33 (0)1 43 26 70 60
www.loubnane.fr

Hungry for some Mediterranean food in Paris? Then why not try some refined Lebanese cuisine. Choose from colourful mezzé and grilled meat and end your meal with the surprisingly good home-made ice-cream of pine resin, orange blossom water and orchid pulp. At Loubnane, Lebanese cuisine is at its finest.

28 MAZEH

65 rue des
Entrepreneurs
A 15 – Invalides &
Eiffel Tower (LB) ⑦
+33 (0)1 45 75 33 89
www.mazeh.com

Mazeh is still one of the best among the many Iranian restaurants, greengrocers and delis on this street. This is where the Iranian community in Paris meets or from where they order their traditional dishes for their parties. The rice flavoured with candied oranges, pistachio or barberries, the typical red berries that are used in Persian cuisine, is a speciality of this restaurant.

29 FOGÓN

45 quai des Grands
Augustins
A 6 – Saint-Germain-
des-Prés & Mont-
parnasse (LB) ⑥
+33 (0)1 43 54 31 33

This elegant restaurant serves all the traditional Spanish dishes but takes a more contemporary and gastronomic approach to the *croquetas*, cured meats and paella. Share some amazing Ibérico de Bellota ham with your table guests, as dictated by tradition. There is a 'Rice' menu for paella fans, which changes depending on the chef's whims and the available produce.

30 UNICO

10 rue Amélie
A 7 – Invalides & Eiffel
Tower (LB) ⑦
+33 (0)1 45 51 83 65
www.resto-unico.com

The vintage Seventies interior of this restaurant is bound to delight fans of Argentine food, as well as anyone who loves a good piece of meat, which they import straight from the Pampas and which is grilled the traditional way over a wood fire. The menu also features a bunch of local specialities like *empanadas*, *lomo* and the quintessential Argentine dessert *'Banana con dulce de leche'*.

29 FOGÓN

The 5 best places for
A WEEKEND BRUNCH

---

31 CLINT

174 rue de la Roquette
A11 – Belleville &
surroundings (RB) ⑨
+33 (0)9 81 60 17 36
*www.clint-restaurant.
com*

Just a short walk from the entrance of
Père Lachaise cemetery this light and airy
restaurant has a soothing ambiance and
atmosphere. Here they don't believe in a
fixed brunch menu but give you the option
of putting together your own from a bunch
of staples including pancakes, scones, eggs
Benedict or home-made granola as well as
burgers if you're ravenous. Pop into the
tiny shop for some groceries before leaving.

32 MAMA SHELTER

109 rue de Bagnolet
A20 – Belleville &
surroundings (RB) ⑨
+33 (0)1 43 48 48 48
www.mamashelter.com

On weekends the brunch buffet at this
alternative boutique hotel is one of the
most popular in the capital. The dishes
change regularly to ensure that everything
looks appetizing, lush and refined. There
is something to suit everyone's tastes,
including a parmentier of duck or Nutella
and whipped cream waffles for the hungry.
If you prefer something healthier then
choose the quinoa salad or a soup. The pace
is leisurely here and you are welcome to
spend the whole afternoon in your club
sofa while the kids gambol around.

33 DERRIÈRE

69 rue des Gravilliers
A3 – Marais & Bastille
(RB) ⑤
+33 (0)1 44 61 91 95
www.derriere-resto.com

This unusual restaurant grew from the idea of receiving people as you would at home. Bambi Sloan, the decorator, converted this warehouse into a quirky and friendly place with an eclectic blend of styles. The Sunday brunch is therefore served in the library or the bedroom where the bed is used as a bench. The highlight of this copious formula definitely is the dessert buffet. Eat without guilt before heading off for a game of ping-pong.

34 MA COCOTTE

106 rue des Rosiers
Saint-Ouen
Montmartre (RB) ⑧
+33 (0)1 49 51 70 00
www.macocotte-lespuces. com

Although this place does not serve a traditional brunch but a series of 'chic snacks' it is the ideal place for a break during a visit to the flea market. Philippe Starck designed this airy and cosy restaurant, combining his own creations with objects from the flea market. There are several dishes for sharing on the menu including Sunday lunch staples like roasted farm chicken for four and comforting desserts for winter weekends.

35 COLORAVA

47 rue de l'Abbé
Grégoire
A6 – Saint-Germain-
des-Prés & Mont-
parnasse (LB) ⑥
+33 (0)1 45 44 67 56

The ideal place for a Sunday lunch for anyone with a sweet tooth or who loves interior design. This patisserie shop and *salon de thé*, which is frequented by the locals of this chic neighbourhood, has two options, from which to choose, which the chef defines as 'a glorious mix of colours and flavours'. The menu features traditional pastries as well as inventive salads, fruit cocktails and the chef's own delectable creations.

5 excellent

ITALIAN

RESTAURANTS

36 **LA TABLE UNIQUE**
LA TÊTE DANS LES OLIVES
2 rue Sainte-Marthe
A 10 – Belleville &
surroundings (RB) ⑨
+33 (0)9 51 31 33 34
lestablesuniques@
latetedanslesolives.com

What a great idea to set just one table in the middle of this tiny and charming delicatessen. At 'La tête dans les olives' you can dine with two or more friends (maximum 6 guests), where you can sample a selection of refined, exceptional Sicilian products, which are prepared for you by the chef. Book well in advance for the privilege of this unique experience.

37 **ASSAPORARE**
7 rue Saint-Nicolas
A 12 – Marais & Bastille
(RB) ⑤
+33 (0)1 44 67 75 77

This discreet restaurant on a quiet street is a local favourite. The owner, Neapolitan Giuseppe Lo Casale, is passionate about food and takes the time to explain the ingredients in every dish in great detail. Expect tomatoes and mozzarella, in a variety of styles and preparations. The menu also includes several Neapolitan specialities. A restaurant that truly delivers happiness.

TICKETS VIA:

38 CIBUS

5 Rue Molière
A 1 – Louvre &
Les Halles (RB) ③
+33 (0)1 42 61 50 19

This tiny restaurant only has six tables. The minimal interior is the perfect backdrop for a special ambiance, making you feel like a member of a privileged club. Because this is where the insiders come to sample dishes that have been made using only organic ingredients, from the oil down to the pasta. The produce is what counts here and the menu is deliberately kept simple to reflect this. Not really a problem because every dish on the menu will simply make you salivate.

39 LE GRAND VENISE

171 rue de la
Convention
A 15 – Invalides &
Eiffel Tower (LB) ⑦
+33 (0)1 45 32 49 71

If you associate Italy with *la dolce vita* and generosity, gilding and gondolas then this is the place to enjoy all this and more. Before dining at Le Grand Venise, we recommend not eating for at least two days. The portions are huge, starting with the delicious antipaste, followed by lasagna and ending on a sweet note with the restaurant's famous home-made caramel ice-cream. A dinner you will be bound to remember.

40 EAST MAMMA

133 rue du Faubourg
Saint-Antoine
A 11 – Marais & Bastille
(RB) ⑤
+33 (0)1 43 41 32 15
*www.bigmamma
group.com*

It's been practically impossible to book a table at this chic and authentic Italian canteen since the day it opened. The enthusiastic kitchen team selects only the best Italian products, which, it must be said, are quite delicious. Traditional dishes like pizza, pasta, antipasti, osso buco and tiramisu are brought to your table by a team of cheerful and friendly waiters.

5 *excellent*
ASIAN RESTAURANTS

---

41 **YAM'TCHA**
121 rue Saint-Honoré
A1 – Louvre & Les
Halles (RB) ③
+33 (0)1 40 26 08 07
www.yamtcha.com

Michelin-starred chef Adeline Grattard is inspired by Chinese cuisine while cherishing her own French heritage, combining Asian elements and French basics and creating the most surprising, delicate and perfumed fusion cuisine. The menus in which she pairs various dishes with different teas make for an unusual tasting experience and the subtlety of these pairings is widely praised.

42 **AU COIN DES GOURMETS**
5 rue Dante
A5 – Quartier Latin
(LB) ④
+33 (0)1 43 26 12 92

This discreet simple Indo-Chinese restaurant is located just a short walk from Notre-Dame. At first glance there is nothing interesting about it. And yet they serve delicious traditional food here. Staples include *nems* or *bobun* as well as some specialities, about which the pleasant waiter waxes downright lyrical. If you are a fan of genuine Asian cuisine, you will love this place.

43 THAÏ ROYAL

97 avenue d'Ivry
A13 – Quartier Latin
(LB) ④
+33 (0)1 44 24 22 11

It is often difficult to choose a good restaurant among the many options available to you in the Chinese district. Thaï Royal is a good choice, serving traditional and creative dishes, which are always beautifully presented. The restaurant's specialities include la gourmandise de Khun Maé which you really should try. These tiny bite-size parcels contain a mixture of grilled coconut, prawns, ginger and lime. A feast for your taste buds.

44 LE PARIS HANOI

74 rue de Charonne
A11 – Marais & Bastille
(RB) ⑤
+33 (0)1 47 00 47 59
www.parishanoi.fr

Le Paris Hanoi is a family affair. This local eatery which was established twenty years ago by three Vietnamese brothers (Mido, Jean Phi and Hando) is such a success nowadays that there is always a line outside the door during peak times, even on rainy days. The menu features various tasty and delicately perfumed traditional Vietnamese dishes, including Pho soups and lemongrass chicken, which you can enjoy in this ever-busy restaurant.

45 LE PETIT CAMBODGE

20 rue Alibert
A10 – Belleville &
surroundings (RB) ⑨
+33 (0)1 42 45 80 88
www.lepetitcambodge.fr

Just a short walk from Canal Saint-Martin this pretty light eatery serves Cambodian specialities as its name indicates. The menu includes several light dishes, like *bobun*, which you can eat in or get to go as well as specialities like *Ban Hoy*, an Angkorian picnic which you can put together yourself. All the produce is fresh, the combinations simply succulent and the atmosphere very pleasant.

45 LE PETIT CAMBODGE

50 KUNITORAYA 1

5 excellent
JAPANESE
RESTAURANTS

---

46 SOLA

12 rue de l' Hôtel-
Colbert
A5 – Quartier Latin
(LB) ④
+33 (0)1 43 29 59 04
www.restaurant-sola.com

The young chef Hiroki Yoshitake has succeeded in creating a graceful fusion of French and Japanese cuisine. In his restaurant Sola he juggles flavours and textures, rewriting the repertoire of cuisine with his airy, visually arresting dishes. His work was rewarded with a Michelin star soon after the opening. Whether you choose to dine in the Japanese dining room or the French dining room with its beams and stonework Sola promises a mind-blowing gastronomic experience.

47 LE GUILO-GUILO

8 rue Garreau
A18 – Montmartre
(RB) ⑧
+33 (0)1 42 54 23 92
www.guiloguilo.com

Dining in this restaurant on Butte-Montmartre is like a ceremony. The first rule is you must reserve several weeks in advance. Once installed at the counter around the kitchen the eight dishes of the one menu, which resemble delicate colourful paintings, are served with reverence, one by one. Start with traditional Japanese dishes and move on to bold creations with surprising flavour combinations.

48 NANASHI

31 rue de Paradis
A 10 – Belleville &
surroundings (RB) ⑨
+33 (0)1 40 22 05 55

This large canteen-grocer's sells 'Parisian bentos'. This consists of a kit with a balanced meal, combining organic vegetables with all sorts of other ingredients with health benefits. The chef, Kaori Endo, pairs market produce with Japanese elements, putting together colourful and copious dishes. The result looks and tastes delicious and fresh, as well as being healthy. But this eatery is so successful that the service can sometimes be lackadaisical.

49 SHABU SHA

72 rue des Gravilliers
A 3 – Marais & Bastille
(RB) ⑤
+33 (0)1 42 77 06 69

The speciality of this restaurant, with its modern and exotic interior, is Japanese fondue. Once you are seated around the main bar, you choose your stock, your sauce and then your waiter will plunge ravioli, noodles, prawns or vegetables into this mixture. Everyone waits while their meal simmers. The perfect place for a fun meal, on your own or with friends.

50 KUNITORAYA 1

5 rue Villedo
A 10 – Louvre &
Les Halles (RB) ③
+33 (0)1 47 03 33 65
www.kunitoraya.com

Kunitoraya is the most popular restaurant among the many Japanese restaurants in this neighbourhood. Sit down at a long communal table, with other habitués and enjoy some of the best udon noodles in Paris. The pleasant waiting staff recommends Tempura-Udon with crispy prawns for novices and Kunitora-Udon for the more advanced.

The 5 best
SANDWICH BARS

---

51 TERROIR PARISIEN

20 rue Saint-Victor
A5 – Quartier Latin
(LB) ④
+33 (0)1 44 31 54 54
www.yannick-alleno.com

Take a seat at the large central counter of this elegant restaurant, whether alone or with a friend, to enjoy a deluxe version of a real Parisian sandwich. Although the price is steep (8 euros!) the sandwich was created by the well-known chef Yannick Alléno using exceptional and locally sourced produce. The copious amounts of just sliced ham combine perfectly with the crunchy bread and the sweet butter. Truly delicious!

52 LE PETIT VENDÔME

8 rue des Capucines
A2 – Arc de Triomphe,
Champs-Élysées &
Grands Boulevards
(RB) ②
+33 (0)1 42 61 05 88

This place stands out in this elegant neighbourhood. At lunch there's a line of people at the counter of this typical con-vivial bistro which is known for its famous *casse-croute auvergnat*. These are baguette sandwiches that are prepared on the spot. Choose from a wide range of garnishes including salami or rillettes but go with the traditional bone-in ham if you want to really have a good sandwich!

53 CHEZ ALINE

85 rue de la Roquette
A11 – Marais & Bastille
(RB) ⑤
+33 (0)1 43 71 90 75

The owner, Delphine Zampetti has preserved almost all the elements of this former horse butcher's from the Fifties, including the yellow tiles and the mica. The *jambon Prince de Paris* sandwich is aptly named. You can eat in or get it to go, but this large sandwich, which has been made with excellent produce and according to the rules of the art perpetuates another great French tradition.

54 CARACTÈRE DE COCHON

42 rue Charlot
A3 – Marais & Bastille
(RB) ⑤
+33 (0)1 42 74 79 45

In the heart of the Marais neighbourhood this lovely *cave à jambon* is a place to remember if you need to quickly assuage your hunger pangs with a sandwich. Take a good look at all the equally delectable types of charcuterie before choosing the star of your sandwich: cured, smoked, cooked, with bergamot… and don't forget the butter: salted or unsalted.

55 LA POINTE DU GROUIN

8 rue de Belzunce
A10 – Montmartre
(RB) ⑧
+33 (0)1 58 78 28 80

This eatery is just a short walk from gare du Nord making it the perfect place to stop just before you hop onto the train. They prepare delicious sandwiches with homemade *ficelle* bread and *charcuterie*, including some excellent ham. Please note that they do not accept euros, here but only the local currency, called *groin*. An original concept and a good topic to start a conversation with your neighbours.

53 CHEZ ALINE

5
exceptional
PATISSERIES

---

56 CYRIL LIGNAC

2 rue de Chaillot
A 16 – Arc de
Triomphe, Champs-
Élysées & Grands
Boulevards (RB) ②
+33 (0)1 47 20 64 51
www.lapatisserie
cyrillignac.com

Cyril Lignac has joined forced with the young pastry chef Benoit Couvrand to open this temple dedicated to delectable sweets. They only sell ten different cakes, choosing to limit the number of options because the ingredients are carefully selected and the fruit is always seasonal. So you will never find a strawberry cake here during the winter months. The traditional pastries with a twist deserve a special mention: a baba au rhum with vanilla whipped cream or a beautifully constructed lemon cake.

57 GÂTEAUX THOUMIEUX

58 rue Saint-
Dominique
A 7 – Invalides &
Eiffel Tower (LB) ⑦
+33 (0)1 45 51 12 12
www.gateaux
thoumieux.com

The Thoumieux adventure continues. First there was the brasserie, then the up-market restaurant and the hotel and now they opened a bakery. Jean-François Piège hired the talented young chef Ludovic Chaussard and chose the themes of sensuality and childhood memories as the main theme for this bakery. India Mahdavi has used pretty pastel colours for the space where you can buy refined pastries like the *Toulousain* or the *Chou-Chou* with salty caramel cream. The place to go for guilt-free pleasures.

58 LA PÂTISSERIE DES MARTYRS

56 CYRIL LIGNAC

58 LA PÂTISSERIE DES MARTYRS

22 rue des Martyrs
A 9 – Montmartre
(RB) ⑧
+33 (0)1 71 18 24 70
www.sebastiengaudard.fr

After earning an excellent reputation for himself at Fauchon among others, Sébastien Gaudard has taken over at the helm of one of the oldest bakeries in Paris. Maison Seurre has recently been renamed La pâtisserie des Martyrs. This lovely store sells all kinds of delicious cakes including *puits d'amour*, *monts-blancs* and *paris-brest* as well as old-fashioned sweets and ice-creams. This virtuoso of sweets is inspired by the desire to perpetuate expertise and put old-fashioned flavours back into the spotlight.

59 PAIN DE SUCRE

14 rue de Rambuteau
A 3 – Marais & Bastille
(RB) ⑤
+33 (0)1 45 74 68 92
www.patisserie paindesucre.com

Nathalie Robert and Didier Mathray, the co-owners of Pain de sucre, which is located in the heart of the Marais district, constant-ly change their range. Their sweet creations include magnificent square cakes (which makes a nice change from tradition), small verrines with bold and tart flavours as well as their divine guimauves or marshmallows which come in 18 different flavours. The Japanese adore visiting this bakery when in Paris!

60 CHEZ BOGATO

7 rue Liancourt
A 14 – Saint-Germain-des-Prés &
Montparnasse
(RB) ⑥
+33 (0)1 40 47 03 51
www.chezbogato.fr

An excellent place to go with children because this bakery and sweet shop is too cute for words. The cakes are simply enchanting and the sweets both ravishing and fun. Enough to make you regress back into your childhood. If you need a stunning birthday cake, then they will rise to the occasion.

The 5 nicest
MARKETS

---

61 **MARCHÉ D'ALIGRE**
Place d'Aligre
A 12 – Marais & Bastille
(RB) ⑤

This market is one of the most diverse markets in the capital, crammed with stalls with organic produce, exotic fruit, Italian and Portuguese products and even some second-hand goods. Don't forget to check out the Grainerie du marché, a tiny quaint shop. You'll find the delis, the butchers and cheese stalls in the covered market. The crowd here is a nice mix of hipsters and working-class people. Open daily except on Monday.

62 **MARCHÉ CONVENTION**
Rue de la Convention
(Entre les rues Alain
Chartier et l'Abbé
Groult)
A 15 – Invalides &
Eiffel Tower (LB) ⑦

This large family-oriented market occupies the entire street. Greengrocers, butchers, fishmongers and cheese sellers… they're all here. The displays are beautifully arranged and the atmosphere is genuinely friendly. Although mums adore this market, which is held three times a week the local restaurant owners also like to visit it because some of the stallholders sell rare vegetables and speciality products. Open on Tuesday, Thursday and Sunday.

63 MARCHÉ BIOLOGIQUE DES BATIGNOLLES

27-48 boulevard des Batignolles
A 17 – Montmartre
(RB) ⑧

Fans of organic food go to this market on Saturday mornings. There are about fifty stallholders, who all grow their own produce for the most part. People appreciate this direct contact without intermediaries, exchanging recipes or cooking tips. This organic market is nicer than the one on Boulevard Raspail, the other organic market on the left bank.

64 MARCHÉ DES ENFANTS ROUGES

9 rue de Beauce
A 3 – Marais & Bastille
(RB) ⑤
+33 (0)1 48 87 80 61

This small market, which is one of the oldest in Paris, is housed in a wooden hall. Although it is not the best market to stock up on fruit and veg it definitely is the place to go for lunch. The tiny restaurants and delis around the market are very popular, especially the Japanese restaurant Taeko and l'Estaminet des Enfants Rouges. Open daily except on Monday.

65 MARCHÉ DU PRÉSIDENT WILSON

Avenue du Président Wilson (entre rue Debrousse et place d'Iéna)
A 16 – Arc de Triomphe, Champs-Élysées & Grands Boulevards (RB) ②

Look no further: this is the chicest market in Paris, it even looks out onto the Eiffel Tower. Japanese tourists who are fascinated with French food rub shoulders with the locals in a slightly artificial atmosphere. But if you like rare and 'old' vegetable varieties then hit up the well-known stall of Joël Thiebault, a star among market gardeners. His display is exceptional and the prices are surprisingly easy on your wallet. Open on Wednesday and Saturday morning.

The 5 most brilliant
BAKERIES

───────

66 DU PAIN ET DES IDÉES

34 rue Yves Toudic
A 10 – Belleville &
surroundings (RB) ⑨
+33 (0)1 42 40 44 52
www.dupainetdesidees.com

This store, which dates from 1870, has managed to retain its charm with its painted glass ceilings and its bevelled mirrors. Christophe Vasseur brought this bakery to life, opening Du pain et des Idées here, which has become very popular. People come from all over Paris for the famous *pain des amis*, the *Mouna brioche* or *la tendresse aux pommes*. A range of authentic products, prepared in accordance with the classic French tradition. The only sour note: the bakery is closed on the weekend.

67 BLÉ SUCRÉ

7 rue Antoine Vollon
A 12 – Marais & Bastille
(RB) ⑤
+33 (0)1 43 40 77 73

The best baguettes are often found in neighbourhood bakeries like at Blé Sucré, a small bakery/pastry shop owned by Fabrice Le Bourdat, who used to work at Hôtel Bristol. The twisted baguette is simply delicious but wait until you've tasted the croissants and the ravishing pastries which are also worth the detour. There are a few tables in front of the shop, facing square Trousseau. The perfect place for a breakfast on the fly.

66 DU PAIN ET DES IDÉES

70 BORIS LUMÉ

68 POILÂNE

8 rue du Cherche-Midi
A6 – Saint-Germain-
des-Prés & Mont-
parnasse (LB) ⑥
+33 (0)1 45 48 42 59
www.poilane.com

Not much has changed since this bakery opened in 1932. The loaves are still hand-fashioned and cooked in a wood-fired oven. And although Poilâne's best known product is its bread, the *Punitions*, tiny buttery crisp cookies, are the bakery's other best-seller. These perfectly round cookies with their scalloped edge are simply inimitable. The charm of the main bakery in Saint-Germain-des-Prés is the perfect setting for a real taste sensation.

69 PANIFICA

15 avenue Trudaine
A9 – Montmartre
(RB) ⑧
+33 (0)1 53 20 91 18

This large traditional bakery sells breads made with organic flour and starter. This traditional commitment to the art of bread making only enhances the bread's taste. Here you will find novelty flavours and fragrances like the pretty dark rye bread (called *tourte de seigle*) or kamut bread. There are a few tables available for breakfast.

70 BORIS LUMÉ

48 rue Caulaincourt
A18 – Montmartre
(RB) ⑧
+33 (0)1 46 06 96 71

This bakery is listed as a historical monument and is owned by a young Franco-Asian couple. It is a must see during any visit to Montmartre. Its postcard setting truly epitomises Paris as everyone knows it but at the same time this bakery is also renowned for its savoir-faire. Everyone adores the traditional baguette but Lumé's pastries like *pain au chocolat* or the *brioche* with almond meal are just as delicious.

The 5 most exceptional
CHOCOLATE SHOPS

—————

71 À LA MÈRE DE FAMILLE

35 rue du Faubourg
Montmartre
A9 – Montmartre
(RB) ⑧
+33 (0)1 47 70 83 69
*www.lameredefamille.
com*

À la Mère de Famille was established in
1761 and is the oldest chocolate shop in
Paris. The historic shop in Faubourg Montmartre is an institution and a landmark for
connoisseurs. The shop sells all kinds of
sweets like guimauve (similar to marshmallows) and old-fashioned sweets as well as
a range of excellent chocolates. The place
to go at Easter, because of the magnificent
eggs, chickens and other tasty creations.

72 À LA PETITE FABRIQUE

12 rue Saint-Sabin
A11 – Marais & Bastille
(RB) ⑤
+33 (0)1 48 05 82 02

This small shop, which is not that well
known but definitely worth visiting, sells
delicious bars of chocolate packed in silver
paper in various colours, at a very reasonable price. The range includes the traditional
almond chocolate, dark chocolate without
sugar (but jam-packed with flavour) for
those who worry about their weight or
even the dark chocolate with matcha tea
for those who prefer a bolder combination.

73 ARNAUD LARHER

53 rue Caulaincourt
A 18 – Montmartre
(RB) ⑧
+33 (0)1 42 57 68 08
www.arnaud-larher.com

This young and discreet chocolate maker opened a shop in Montmartre and received various awards inlcuding that of *Meilleur Ouvrier* (best craftsman) in France as well as an award from the *Club des Croqueurs de Chocolat*, a well-known French institution, for best chocolate makers. His chocolate bars are extremely refined and people with a sweet tooth have been known to travel across Paris to his shop for his delicious sweets with black ganache and an infusion of wild pepper or thyme.

74 LA MANUFACTURE DE CHOCOLAT

40 rue de la Roquette
A11 – Marais & Bastille
(RB) ⑤
+33 (0)1 48 05 82 86
www.lechocolat-alainducasse.com

You can smell the chocolate from the street. The chocolate factory of the famous French chef Alain Ducasse can be found at the back of the courtyard, in a renovated factory. This transparent and lively place reveals all the secrets and techniques of the complex and exciting process of chocolate making. Everyone can look in. The products are wrapped in delightful packaging and displayed like tiny art works.

75 JEAN-PAUL HÉVIN

231 rue Saint-Honoré
A 1 – Arc de Triomphe,
Champs-Élysées &
Grands Boulevards
(RB) ②
+33 (0)1 55 35 35 96
www.jeanpaulhevin.com

This exceptional chocolate maker travels all over the world, bringing back special cocoa beans from some of the best plantations in the world. Sweets, pralines, pastries, chocolate bars or fun creations for the holidays, Hévin has it all. Chocolate fans will find it hard to resist this master craftsman's delicate and subtle products (especially the dark chocolate). Hévin's chocolates are appreciated by the public and his peers alike.

Outside Paris => 2 coffee
La Chocolatiere Royale -
Orleans 51 rue Royale
www.lachocolatiere45.com

57

5 superb
GREENGROCERS

---

76 **G. DETOU**

58 rue Tiquetonne
A 2 – Louvre &
Les Halles (RB) ③
+33 (0)1 42 36 54 67

This timeless grocery with its evocative name is a favourite with amateur and professional bakers. Here you will all the ingredients you need, even the rarest, including chocolate chips, gold leaf, pralines or natural flavours, for that wonderful cake you are making. This place is an institution that has managed to retain its soul.

77 **GOUMANYAT BY THIERCELIN**

3 rue Charles-François
Dupuis
A 3 – Marais & Bastille
(RB) ⑤
+33 (0)1 44 78 96 74
www.thiercelin1809.com

A must visit for discerning gourmets and anyone wishing to impress his or her guests with some exceptional dishes. Tasmanian pepper, Tahitian vanilla, Himalayan pink salt, rose petals from Damascus… all these products have been hand-picked by the shop's owners, who have specialised in rare ingredients since 1809. Today they ship these ingredients to Paris to delight our palate and satisfy our curiosity.

78 **IZRAEL**

30 rue François Miron
A 4 – Marais & Bastille
(RB) ⑤
+33 (0)1 42 72 66 23

Izrael is a big favourite with foodies and anyone who is lured in by the window display of this Ali Baba's cave full of candied fruit, a multitude of different spices and specialities from North Africa, Israel and China. Here everything is so tantalising that you will come back for more. You can find pistachios from Iran here, as well as tonka beans or rare mustards. A visit to the shop is like a voyage around the world.

79 RAP

4 rue Fléchier
A 9 – Montmartre
(RB) ⑧
+33 (0)1 42 80 09 91
www.rapparis.fr

While it is true that there are many Italian grocery stores in Paris the authenticity of the products they sell is sometimes less reliable. At RAP you can buy with confidence as they source their cheeses, olive oils and tomato sauces directly from local producers. This grocery store is also a great meeting place as the owner, Alessandra Pierini, regularly organises cooking workshops and wine tastings in the presence of the wine producers.

80 LES ENFANTS GÂTÉS

6bis rue des Récollets
A 10 – Belleville &
surroundings (RB) ⑨
+33 (0)9 81 41 38 36

This lovely little grocery near canal Saint-Martin is full of exceptional products from all over France and the world. It is the perfect place to put together a refined picnic, with Portuguese sardines, Gouda cheese with truffle from Bordier, Goutte d'Or beers that are brewed in the 18th Arrondissement and many other rare products.

Chocolate- Josephine Vannier
4 rue du Pas-de-la-Mule
www.chocolates-
vannier.com

---

81 LE BONBON AU PALAIS

19 rue Monge
A5 – Quartier Latin
(LB) ④
+33 (0)1 78 56 15 72
www.bonbonsaupalais.fr

Georges, the passionate owner of this unusual shop, invites you to take a journey back into your childhood. He has selected sweets from some of the best craftsmen and confectioners in France and sells a range of old-fashioned sweets like *berlingots*, fruit jellies, fresh *guimauves* (marshmallows), nougat and other regional specialities. The mix of colours and flavours is so overwhelming that you will not be able to resist the lure of this shop.

82 ROELLINGER

51 rue Sainte-Anne
A2 – Louvre &
Les Halles (RB) ③
+33 (0)1 42 60 46 88
*www.epices-
roellinger.com*

Here's an address that gourmets will appreciate. Olivier Roellinger selects spices and condiments from some of the most beautiful gardens in the world. He creates subtle blends with evocative names like *poudre des alizés* to add to a dressing, *poudre des fées* to spice up a soup or *poudre défendue* to enhance a strawberry salad.

83 SOU QUAN

35 place Maubert
A5 – Quartier Latin
(LB) ④
+33 (0)1 43 26 80 39

This pocket-sized grocery store sells all the basic ingredients you need to prepare traditional Asian dishes. These include exotic fruit and vegetables, as well as various types of rice, noodles, spices and sauces. This tiny place in the centre of Paris is a firm favourite with home cooks and restaurant owners.

Breizh Café + Creperie
109 rue Vieille du Temple
www.breizhcafe.com

84 MMMOZZA

57 rue de Bretagne
A3 – Marais & Bastille
(RB) ⑤
+33 (0)1 42 71 82 98

This tiny deli has specialised in mozzarella, but the kind of mozzarella that does not in any way resemble the industrial product of the same name. Laura Vestrucci originally hails from Florence. She wants the people of Paris to rediscover the taste of this iconic Italian product. *Di bufala*, *burrata* or smoked… She gladly explains the various subtleties and pairings.

85 LA TÊTE DANS LES OLIVES

2 rue Sainte-Marthe
A10 – Belleville &
surroundings (RB) ⑨
+33 (0)9 51 31 33 34
www.latetedanslesolives.com

This tiny shop imports all its products from Sicily including salted capers, sun-dried figs, fennel seeds as well as extraordinary extra virgin olive oils which they source from small family-owned olive farms. The owner Cédric Casanova monitors every step of the production process, from the olive groves to the mills and sells a range of oils that is so intense and has such a delicate and varied flavour that it will be hard to resist buying just one bottle.

81 LE BONBON AU PALAIS

5 indispensable
CHEESE SHOPS

---

86 FROMAGERIE GRIFFON

23bis avenue de la Motte Picquet
A7 – Invalides & Eiffel Tower (LB) ⑦
+33 (0)1 45 50 14 85
fromagerie-griffon.com

Young Claire Griffon opened this elegant and luxurious cheese shop which sells exceptional products that she sources from small French producers. The star products here are aged mimolette and a comté grand cru but do also try some of her other refined and tasty creations.

87 BARTHÉLÉMY

51 rue de Grenelle
A7 – Saint-Germain-des-Prés & Montparnasse (LB) ⑥
+33 (0)1 42 22 82 24

The owner, an iconic cheese seller, treats all the cheeses in his shop with love. He supplies to the Élysée Palace among others. Here the cheese is matured to perfection and as is the case with fruit and vegetables, we recommend following the seasons. A goat cheese, reblochon or camembert for example are traditionally eaten in the summertime.

88 ALLÉOSSE

13 rue Poncelet
A17 – Arc de Triomphe, Champs-Élysées & Grands Boulevards (RB) ②
+33 (0)1 46 22 50 45
www.fromage-alleosse.com

Philippe Alléosse and his wife are the current generation in a long line of master cheesemongers. They age their cheese in their own cellars in the centre of Paris according to their own traditional method. Their aim is to reveal the flavours and aromas of soft and hard cheeses. Although theirs is a very rigorous and demanding profession they take special care of their window display, combining various shapes and colours.

89 LAURENT DUBOIS

97-99 rue Saint-
Antoine
A 4 – Marais & Bastille
(RB) ⑤
+33 (0)1 48 87 17 10
*www.fromages
laurentdubois.fr*

In his tiny shop in quartier Saint-Paul, this cheesemonger who has been named best craftsman of France, sells a high-end selection of cheese and butter. Follow the staff's excellent advice and be tempted by seasonal cheeses and other marvellous cheese products.

90 FROMAGERIE QUATREHOMME

62 rue de Sèvres
A 7 – Invalides &
Eiffel Tower (LB) ⑦
+33 (0)1 47 34 33 45
www.quatrehomme.fr

This family-owned cheesemonger's, which opened in 1953, is currently run by Marie Quatrehomme, who was voted best craftsman of France. It is one of the most reputable cheese shops in the capital. Cheese lovers flock here for the Vacherin Mont d'Or with truffle and goat cheese that has aged 100 days. Both of these cheeses require careful ripening.

5 places to sample

A DELICIOUS CHARCUTERIE PLATE

91 COINSTOT VINO

26bis passage des
Panoramas
A2 – Louvre &
Les Halles (RB) ③
+33 (0)1 44 82 08 54
www.coinstot-vino.com

This place is located in the centre of the passage des panoramas, one of the oldest in Paris and serves up some excellent charcuterie. You can enjoy your cold cuts on a terrace, away from the hustle and bustle of the city, along with a glass of their selection of natural wines.

92 LA TRINQUETTE

67 Rue des Gravilliers
A3 – Marais & Bastille
(RB) ⑤
+33 (0)9 52 07 80 60

Lean on a barrel or on the bar in this wine bar in the Marais while you enjoy a selection of charcuterie in a festive and friendly atmosphere. The owners will recommend which wine goes best with your cold cuts. On weekends we recommend coming early because this bar tends to get very busy.

93 TERRA CORSA

42 rue des Martyrs
A9 – Montmartre
(RB) ⑧
+33 (0)1 48 78 20 70

This lovely deli/table d'hôtes serves large portions of Corsican charcuterie which you can share. Wild boar sausage and *lonzo* pair nicely with the wines from the pretty island. You can also shop for some of the best regional specialities here.

94 JEANNE B

61 rue Lepic
A 18 – Montmartre
(RB) ⑧
+33 (0)1 42 51 17 53
www.jeanne-b-
comestibles.com

This grocery/rotisserie with its contemporary and warm interior offers a nice selection of charcuterie and traditional cheeses. Far from the tourist traps this place is the ideal place to sit down before or after your walk through Montmartre. Jeanne B also serves dinner and caters parties.

95 GILLES VÉROT

7 rue Lecourbe
A 15 – Invalides &
Eiffel Tower (LB) ⑦
+33 (0)1 47 34 01 03
www.verot-charcuterie.fr

If you're considering a picnic then head over to the shop of Gilles Vérot, probably the best butcher in Paris. Some of the shop's bestsellers include bone-in ham, head cheese and *paté en croûte*. A must for all fans of good charcuterie.

94 JEANNE B

The 5 best
HAMBURGER JOINTS

96 SCHWARTZ'S DELI

7 avenue d'Eylau
A 16 – Invalides &
Eiffel Tower (LB) ⑦
+33 (0)1 47 04 73 61
www.schwartzsdeli.fr

Yes, it feels like New York and yet you're only a short walk away from place du Trocadéro. Here you can enjoy various staples of North American cuisine as well as the deli's renowned and tasty hamburgers. Whether you order the Yankee Burger or the Veggie Burger, they are equally copious. And a good thing too because once you sit down you will start to feel those hanger pangs. It goes without saying that there is a line…

97 BLEND

1 boulevard des Filles
du Calvaire
A 3 – Marais & Bastille
(RB) ⑤
blendhamburger.com

Why do people think of hamburgers as junk food? At Blend they serve 'gourmet burgers', made with hand-shaped rolls, 100% pure beef sourced from the best butcher in Paris (Yves-Marie Le Bourdonnec) and home-made ketchup. Blend's signature burger is made with bleu d'auvergne AOP and emmental de Savoie: all the best of France, combined in one burger!

98 BIG FERNAND

32 rue Saint-Sauveur
A 2 – Louvre &
Les Halles (RB) ③
+33 (0)9 67 22 40 06
www.bigfernand.com

This burger chef serves custom burgers with the meat, cheese, sauce and even the herbs of your choice, along with *fermandines*, the restaurant's home-made French fries. So many reasons to return to this hamburger restaurant where every burger is served with a smile.

99 HAND

39 rue de Richelieu
A1 – Louvre &
Les Halles (RB) ③
+33 (0)1 40 15 03 27

The restaurant HAND (an acronym of Have A Nice Day) was one of the figureheads of the American diner trend well before the other new places that opened more recently in Paris. We like to go there for the selection of burgers as well as for the setting because the interior decoration is quite fun too. The friendly waiters add to the place's cheery atmosphere.

100 JOE ALLEN

30 rue Pierre Lescot
A1 – Louvre &
Les Halles (RB) ③
+33 (0)1 42 36 70 13
www.joeallenparis.com

This place is an institution. Joe Allen opened in 1972 in the Halles neighbourhood and is the oldest American restaurant in Paris. Burger fans and New Yorkers who miss home converge in this typical burger joint, with photos of Hollywood stars on the exposed red brick walls. Joe Allen is the place to go with a large group of friends or family.

97 BLEND

5 spots
for a good
BREAKFAST

---

101 LE MOULIN DE LA VIERGE

10 place des Petits Pères
A2 – Louvre &
Les Halles (RB) ③
+33 (0)1 42 60 02 78
www.lavierge.com

Since 1974 Basile Kamir has worked hard to maintain the sense of authenticity in his Parisian bakeries. The new bakery, which is listed as a historical monument, is located in quiet place des Petits Pères. It has a gorgeous bakery/pastry shop as well as a tiny café. There are a few tables on the terrace where you can enjoy a traditional breakfast with a view of Notre Dame des Victoires.

102 LA RÉGALADE CONSERVATOIRE

7-9 rue du
Conservatoire
A9 – Montmartre
(RB) ⑧
+33 (0)1 44 83 83 60
www.hoteldenell.com

La Régalade Conservatoire in Hôtel de Nell, a five-star chic yet casual hotel, is located in the heart of the 9th Arrondissement and is a pleasant place where you can discuss confidential matters over a delicious breakfast. The restaurant serves a delicious traditional breakfast prepared with a range of high-quality products sourced from some of the best craftsmen in the capital.

103 MAISON KARRENBAUER

11 rue de Charonne
A11 – Marais & Bastille
(RB) ⑤
+33 (0)1 48 05 83 76

This shop was established in 1896 in Lorraine but opened a second branch in Paris. Enter this tiny bar which resembles a confectioner's shop with old-fashioned sweets on display and you will be overcome with nostalgia. Enjoy a breakfast of beautiful traditional pastries in the quaint breakfast room or on the tiny terrace.

104 FRENCHIE TO GO

9 rue du Nil
A 2 – Louvre &
Les Halles (RB) ③
frenchietogo.com

After opening a restaurant and a wine bar the talented chef Gregory Marchand opened a luxury deli. There is a distinctly Anglo-Saxon feel to the breakfast here, which includes delicious muffins, scones with bacon and maple syrup or sticky buns, which are served at the counter. The cheery mood of the young staff will help you start the day off right.

105 CLAUS

14 rue Jean-Jacques
Rousseau
A 1 – Louvre &
Les Halles (RB) ③
+33 (0)1 42 33 55 10
www.clausparis.com

If you like a balanced but delicious breakfast then head over to Claus. Here they only serve organic products that are hand-picked by the owner, as well as the house's specialities, in a light and cosy setting. A lighter alternative to the traditional Parisian breakfast of croissants and sandwiches with butter.

Rose Bakery - quiche
46 Rue des Martyrs (9th)
30 Rue Debelleyme (3rd)

5

COOKING CLASSES
to check out

106 LE CORDON BLEU

8 rue Léon Delhomme
A 15 – Invalides &
Eiffel Tower (LB) ⑦
+33 (0)1 53 68 22 50
www.lcbparis.com

This world-famous school offers cooking courses for amateurs. The *Le marché de Paris* course is especially successful. You visit the market with a chef who teaches you how to choose the best products. Shopping is followed by a snack and a demo during the chef teaches you how to prepare a seasonal menu. (Course in English.)

107 ATELIER GUY MARTIN

35-37 rue Miromesnil
A 8 – Arc de Triomphe,
Champs-Élysées &
Grands Boulevards
(RB) ②
+33 (0)1 42 66 33 33
*www.atelierguymartin.
com*

The cooking school of the Michelin-starred chef of the mythical Grand Véfour restaurant is located in a mansion in the chic 8th Arrondissement. Over lunch you can choose from the *Cours sur le pouce* option, which includes a class and a tasting. Probably one of the best classes available in Paris. For 19 euros you learn a seasonal recipe in half an hour, which can be easily reproduced at home. The course is followed by a tasting in the kitchen or on the small patio where you share your meal with the other course members. A soothing and informative experience.

108 PAROLE IN CUCINA

5 impasse du Curé
A18 – Belleville &
surroundings (RB) ⑨
+33 (0)1 55 79 19 13
www.paroleincucina.com

Sicilian Alba Pezone has managed to get rid of her homesickness by inviting Italy to her table. Ten years ago she decided to share her passion for fine cuisine with others opening a cooking school in a beautifully renovated printers' in the 18th Arrondisse-ment. While her courses on the specialities of the big cities like Florence and Palermo are simply mouth-watering, the ones on pizza or fresh pasta are simply indispen-sable to learn the essentials of Italian gastronomy.

109 PARIS HANOI LABORATOIRE

9 rue Mont-Louis
A11 – Belleville &
surroundings (RB) ⑨
+33 (0)7 60 54 08 48
www.parishanoi.fr

After the success of their restaurants the three brothers opened a space that is dedicated to the discovery of Vietnamese cuisine. In this old converted carpenter's workshop you can learn how to cook Viet-namese dishes. The course focuses on sig-nature dishes like fresh spring rolls, subtle lemongrass chicken or the delicate *bobun*. We cannot think of a better place to learn Vietnamese daily cuisine where tradition and modernity are combined.

110 COOKERY SCHOOL ALAIN DUCASSE

64 rue du Ranelagh
A16
+33 (0)1 44 90 91 00
www.ecolecuisine-alainducasse.com

Celebrated chef Alain Ducasse offers so many different courses in his cookery school that everyone will find their perfect match, however (in)experienced they are and whatever their goal is. Whether you want to learn how to prepare the perfect bistro dish, or how to master specific tech-niques, how to cook light and healthy or how to become the perfect *pâtissier*, Alain Ducasse's team, trained in his restaurants, will help you out. Some courses are taught in English.

5
inspiring
TEA ROOMS

---

111 LA MAISON DE LA CHINE

76 rue Bonaparte
A6 – Saint-Germain-des-Prés & Mont-parnasse (LB) ⑥
+33 (0)1 40 51 95 17
www.maisondelachine.fr

La Maison de la Chine is where you will find fans of Asia in Paris, as well as this tea room which is well-known among insiders. Although it may seem rather strange to have tea at a travel agents' it is even stranger to have a tea in combination with cheese. This unusual combination however is worth trying. Here they serve Fourme d'Ambert with Lapsang Souchong.

112 LA GRANDE MOSQUÉE DE PARIS

39 rue Saint-Hilaire
A5 – Quartier Latin (LB) ④
+33 (0)1 43 31 38 20
www.la-mosquee.com

Do you feel like a mint tea, some oriental pastries, do you need an escape? Then sit down on the patio of this impressive Moorish style mosque which was built in the Twenties. It may remind you of a Moroccan riad with its blue mosaics, the fountain and the plantings. Parisians love to come here, especially on sunny days, so try to come at off-peak times, for example in the morning.

113 LILY OF THE VALLEY

12 rue Dupetit-Thouars
A3 – Marais & Bastille (RB) ⑤
+33 (0)1 57 40 82 80

This tiny tearoom in the Marais neighbourhood is the perfect spot to meet up with your girlfriends around teatime. From the ceiling covered in floral patterns made from recycled fabric from old sofas, up to the English high tea arrangement, everything about this place is sweet and feminine. The choice of teas and the cakes only add to the nice, soft atmosphere.

114 CARETTE

25 place des Vosges
A3 – Marais & Bastille
(RB) ⑤
+33 (0)1 48 87 94 07

This mythical Parisian tea room which was established in 1927 opened a second branch in the Marais overlooking place des Vosges. The menu includes several classic French pastries as well as an amazing selection of teas and hot drinks. Although the atmosphere can feel a bit stilted the location and the refined service are timelessly good.

115 MUSÉE DE LA VIE ROMANTIQUE

16 rue Chaptal
A9 – Montmartre
(RB) ⑧
+33 (0)1 55 31 95 67
*www.paris.fr/pratique/
musees-expos/musee-de-
la-vie-romantique/p5851*

At the end of the paved alleyway which leads to this tiny museum you will notice a pretty house with green shutters. The bucolic setting and the tranquillity of this place portend a nice surprise. Next to the house there is a greenhouse at the end of the shaded courtyard full of flowers, with garden furniture. It seems as if you are no longer in the city. This *buvette* is an enchanting place for a break with a tea from the famous Parisian brand Angelina along with a pastry. Good to know: the refreshment area is only open from April to October.

Mariage Freres : Maison de
The à Paris
Marais - 30·32·35 rue du
Bourg-Tibourg
17 place de la Madeleine
www. Mariage.freres.com

The 5 best
SPECIALITY RESTAURANTS

116 BALLS

47 rue Saint-Maur
A 11 – Belleville &
surroundings (RB) ⑨
+33 (0)9 51 38 74 89
www.ballsrestaurant.com

As its name indicates this restaurant only serves meatballs. This new concept in Paris was dreamed up by Salomé and Jérémie. The tiny spheres, which you can find on plates from Scandinavia to North Africa, in a meaty or vegetarian version, come with a sauce and an assortment of your choice, served on an enamel dish. Effective and above all filling!

117 MAISON F

3 rue Rougemont
A 9 – Louvre &
Les Halles (RB) ③
+33 (0)1 42 46 23 16
www.maison-f.com

Maison F pays tribute to the French fry in all its incarnations, including *allumettes*, the traditional fry or the steak fry. Using different potato varieties, cooking fats and seasonings the bestselling product of this restaurant can be had in a variety of forms in a warm and contemporary setting. An unique concept for France, but which has received the seal of approval from purists.

118 LE GYOZA BAR

56 passage des
Panoramas
A 2 – Louvre &
Les Halles (RB) ③
+33 (0)1 44 82 00 62
gyozabar.com

Sit down at the counter where you can watch the chef at work for a plate of *gyoza*, the iconic steamed Japanese ravioli. This original and fun formula is ideal if you feel a bit hungry or are eating on a budget. Served per 8 or 12, with rice or marinated soy.

119 AUX MERVEILLEUX DE FRED

2 rue Monge
A5 - Quartier Latin
(LB) ④
+33 (0)1 43 54 63 72
www.auxmerveilleux.com

The simplest ideas are often the best.
A proverb which is perfectly suited to the
merveilleux, the delicious meringues that are
covered with whipped cream and which
are a traditional staple in northern France
and Flanders. Chef Frédéric Vaucamps sells
his take on this pastry, having developed
six different flavours, available in three
different sizes (mini, individual, or as a
cake for sharing). Only very few customers
succeed in resisting the deliciously airy
merveilleux.

120 L'ÉCLAIR DE GÉNIE

14 rue Pavée
A4 - Marais & Bastille
(RB) ⑤
+33 (0)1 42 77 85 11
www.leclairdegenie.com

This bakery specialises in éclairs, selling an
infinite array of this best-selling pastry. The
chef Christophe Adam combines different
flavours and shapes, combining delicate or
bolder flavours. Choose from traditional
éclairs with a *grand cru* chocolate or éclairs
with a hazelnut praline. Or maybe you
will plump for the seasonal éclairs, such as
strawberry or yuzu and lemon.

119 AUX MERVEILLEUX DE FRED

CAVES LEGRAND

45 PLACES
FOR A DRINK

5 unusual places
TO HAVE A DRINK

---

121 MARIN D'EAU DOUCE

Embarquement basin
de la Villette
37 quai de Seine
A 19 – Belleville &
surroundings (RB) ⑨
+33 (0)1 42 09 54 10
www.marindeaudouce.fr

Here's a great alternative for the popular but touristy bateaux mouches: you can rent a small electric boat (a sailor's permit isn't necessary) and sail around the canals of Paris at your own pace, just following your nose. There are baskets available to take with you on the boat, filled with a wide choice of appetizers: perfect for a small cruise with friends, a romantic getaway or a family outing. Marin d'eau douce has everything you need to make your search for the hidden secrets of Paris as pleasant as can be.

122 LE CHINA CLUB

50 rue de Charenton
A 12 – Marais & Bastille
(RB) ⑤
+33 (0)1 43 46 08 09
www.lechina.eu

This house with its pretty flowery façade is home to one of the most unusual places in the capital. The atmosphere is Shanghai in the Thirties. Sit down in one of the Chesterfield sofas, alone, with one or several friends and order one of the infamous cocktails with exotic names, such as 'Fleur de Chine' or the 'Chinese Mojito'. Enjoy your brief escape to Asia.

123 MINI PALAIS

3 avenue Winston
Churchill
A 8 – Arc de Triomphe,
Champs-Élysées &
Grands Boulevards
(RB) ②
+33 (0)1 42 56 42 42
www.minipalais.com

The 'Mini Palais' restaurant and bar is located in the area between Champs Élysées and pont Alexandre III in the left wing of Grand Palais. The terrace is surrounded by huge stone columns, sculptures and palm trees. Petit Palais is just across the way. The prestigious and historical setting makes this one of the most chic and exclusive venues in Paris.

124 PÂTISSERIE CIEL

3 rue Monge
A 5 – Quartier Latin
(LB) ④
+33 (0)1 43 29 40 78
www.patisserie-ciel.com

This Japanese pastry shop is renowned for its Angel Cakes. These delicate pastries are as light as a cloud. They also serve champagne and Japanese whiskeys. In the evening you can choose a menu which pairs Japanese food with cocktails. We recommend going here alone or with a friend for an intimate, refined and unusual experience. The number of places at the counter is limited (only 8!).

125 LA GARE

19 chaussée de la
Muette
A 16
+33 (0)1 42 15 15 31
restaurantlagare.com

Passy La Muette station now has a restaurant and bar. The building was built along the railway line of the *Petite Ceinture* and opened in 1854. The young and beautiful as well as the locals like the colonial feel of this amazing setting, which has been redesigned by the architect Laura Gonzalez, coming here for drinks at the bar or on the sun-drenched green terrace.

5

COCKTAIL BARS

---

126 EXPÉRIMENTAL COCKTAIL CLUB

37 rue Saint-Sauveur
A2 – Louvre &
Les Halles (RB) ③
+33 (0)1 45 08 88 09
*www.experimental
cocktailclub.com*

The Expérimental Cocktail Club launched the trend of cocktail bars in Paris. The cosy atmosphere is perfect for sampling some signature cocktails or mixes based on rare spirits, fresh fruit juice and spices. They also invite DJs so you can party into the night.

127 L'ENTRÉE DES ARTISTES PIGALLE

30-32 rue Victor Massé
A9 – Montmartre
(RB) ⑧
+33 (0)9 67 27 37 44
*www.lentree
desartistespigalle.com*

This cocktail bar already has a well-established reputation: the drinks you can order here, some of them classics, others experimental, are among the most famous in the city. The bar has everything you need for a night out in a velvety décor. Start buy ordering a cocktail on the ground floor and then move upstairs to enjoy some sophisticated food.

128 LITTLE RED DOOR

60 rue Charlot
A3 – Marais & Bastille
(RB) ⑤
+33 (0)1 42 71 19 32
www.lrdparis.com

Behind this tiny red door is a very popular yet clandestine cocktail bar. This place has become the headquarters of the trendy young crowd, which likes the style of this place because it resembles a New York loft. Here they can taste cocktails by some of the best mixologists. It does get very crowded here very quickly and as a result the Little Red Door is well on its way to becoming an institution.

129 **ARTISAN**

14 rue Bochart de
Saron
A9 – Montmartre
(RB) ⑧
+33 (0)1 48 74 65 38
artisan-bar.fr

The soothing ambiance of this place is a
nice alternative to the dark cocktail bars
that often can feel too overdone. The young
creative mixologists prepare an array of
cocktails, which are paired with excellent
dishes with seasonal ingredients that are
served around the large U-shaped bar. The
kitchen is open late. This place will definitely appeal to fans of refined flavours and
a more serene atmosphere.

130 **LE CANDELARIA**

52 rue de Saintonge
A3 – Marais & Bastille
(RB) ⑤
+33 (0)1 42 74 41 28
www.candelariaparis.com

This *taqueria* which serves tacos and
guacamole in the Marais is all the rage at
the moment. This is largely the merit of
its intimate and cosy cocktail bar which
is hidden in the back room. The original
creations of the bar tenders such as the infamous *Guêpe Verte* (Green Wasp) with Ocho
blanco tequila which has been infused with
chilli, cucumber, coriander, agave and lime
is your ticket for an explosive and exotic
journey.

5

PALATIAL BARS

---

131 PARK HYATT PARIS VENDÔME

5 rue de la Paix
A 2 – Arc de Triomphe,
Champs-Élysées &
Grands Boulevards
(RB) ②
+33 (0)1 58 71 12 34
*www.paris.vendome.
hyatt.com*

In the late afternoon the regulars enjoy the intimacy and the comfort of this bar, which is perfectly suited for a business meeting. In the early evening, however, the atmosphere changes. The light is dimmed and the ballet of bar tenders starts. The prestigious menu will appeal to even the most discerning palate: cocktails, a selection of excellent wines and champagnes as well as exceptional spirits like the Louis XIII, an Armagnac from 1902 and rare liqueurs and other spirits, including a magnificent collection of Chartreuse.

132 FOUR SEASONS HÔTEL GEORGE V

31 avenue George V
A 8 – Arc de Triomphe,
Champs-Élysées &
Grands Boulevards
(RB) ②
+33 (0)1 49 52 70 00
*www.fourseasons.com/
paris/*

With its wood panelling, its magnificent chandelier, its English Regency sofas and side tables and the fireplace in the corner the bar at the Four Seasons Hôtel George V is a welcoming albeit traditional setting. The perfect place for a discreet meeting or an intimate conversation. You can also have lunch here. Don't forget to try their signature cocktail, called Blurred Lines.

133 PRINCE DE GALLES

33 avenue George V
A8 – Arc de Triomphe,
Champs-Élysées &
Grands Boulevards
(RB) ②
+33 (0)1 53 23 77 77
*www.princedegalles
paris.com*

If you are looking for a relaxing stopover in green surroundings then the patio of this palace is the perfect place for you. Winter and summer people come here to enjoy a good cigar and some amazing cocktails. The most requested drinks are the Mojito Thai, made with Thai basil leaves and ginger, and the Parisian Smash, a blend of whisky, liqueur and passion fruit, which is served in a pretty vial which you pour over a scoop of ice-cream.

134 LE ROYAL MONCEAU

37 avenue Hoche
A8 – Arc de Triomphe,
Champs-Élysées &
Grands Boulevards
(RB) ②
+33 (0)1 42 99 88 00
*www.leroyalmonceau.
com*

This luxurious new-style hotel, which was redesigned from top to bottom by Philippe Starck is all about art and creation. The bar includes 'the barman's cocktail' on its menu. Tell the barman your preferences in terms of fruit or flavours and he will custom mix a cocktail for you, which you can enjoy at the bar or on the terrace.

135 LE MEURICE

228 rue de Rivoli
A1 – Arc de Triomphe,
Champs-Élysées &
Grands Boulevards
(RB) ②
+33 (0)1 44 58 10 10
*www.dorchester
collection.com*

Bar 228 at the hôtel Le Meurice is an institution. The plush setting is the home of the head barman, William Oliveri. We recommend following his excellent advice. Among the 300 options on the menu the Bellini they serve here, a famous Venetian cocktail made with champagne and peach purée, is probably one of the best in Paris.

5 bars to
'SEE AND BE SEEN'

136 PAUSE CAFÉ

41 rue de Charonne
A11 – Marais & Bastille
(RB) ⑤
+33 (0)1 48 06 80 33

From breakfast to the cocktail hour the large terrace of Pause Café is invaded by a crowd of thirty-somethings, a mix of locals, actors and young parents. This pretty café which was used as the setting for Cédric Klapisch's film *Chacun cherche son chat* is a strategic meeting point for anyone who lives in the east of Paris.

137 LA PERLE

78 rue Vieille du
Temple
A3 – Marais & Bastille
(RB) ⑤
+33 (0)1 42 72 69 93
cafelaperle.com

La Perle continues to be a favourite meeting place. At first glance this looks like yet another ordinary café. That said, its faded Seventies decoration, its centrally placed bar where you can enjoy a coffee on the fly and the few tables on the pavement outside attract models, artists, party-goers and locals. Against all odds, this Parisian melting pot has a friendly, relaxed atmosphere.

138 CHEZ JEANNETTE

47 rue du Faubourg
Saint-Denis
Arr 10 – Belleville &
surroundings (RB) ⑨
+33 (0)1 47 70 30 89
chezjeannette.com

This bar is an institution in this working-class cosmopolitan street. The decoration is retro and the lively atmosphere attracts the artists of the neighbourhood: architects, graphic designers, filmmakers… they all meet here as soon as the door opens. But the peak time comes at the end of the day because the regulars like to meet here before going out. Fun if you like a joyful crowd.

139 CAFÉ CHARLOT

38 rue de Bretagne
A3 – Marais & Bastille
(RB) ⑤
+33 (0)1 44 54 03 30
www.cafecharlotparis.com

In this famous street in the Marais this former bakery which has been converted into a bar-restaurant is impossible to miss. The strategically placed large terrace makes Charlot the perfect place for some amazing people watching as all the hipsters of Paris stroll by. In the early evening it can be very busy here so go in the morning if you want to experience the real atmosphere.

140 AUX DEUX AMIS

45 rue Oberkampf
A11 – Belleville &
surroundings (RB) ⑨
+33 (0)1 58 30 38 13

You may walk past this tiny bar with its simple decoration and just a few tables on the pavement. But the simplicity of this place is what makes it so interesting. In just a few years this has become the place to be in rue Oberkampf. You'll find the local BoHos here at all times of the day. Foodies also like to visit this place for its menu of revamped traditional dishes and the amazing wine list.

SUN-DRENCHED TERRACES

141 PLACE DU MARCHÉ SAINTE-CATHERINE

Rue Caron
A4 – Marais & Bastille
(RB) ⑤

If you are looking for a quiet place away from the bustling city, then head to this tiny tree-lined square, with its many public benches. It is the perfect place to meet with friends because of its location in the heart of the Marais. Many of the bars and restaurants set up tables in the square during the day. A good place for an early morning coffee or afternoon and evening drinks, rather than a meal.

142 L'EBOUILLANTÉ

6 rue des Barres
A4 – Marais & Bastille
(RB) ⑤
+33 (0)1 42 74 70 52
www.restaurant-ebouillante.fr

Just a short walk from the church of Saint-Gervais-Saint-Protais in a narrow cobbled street you will find one of the prettiest terraces in Paris. The blue façade, the garden chairs and the parasols immediately make you feel as if you are on holiday. The lunch and dinner menu features *Dînettes*, large salads or daily specials. We recommend coming on weekdays or during off-peak times.

143 LE SAUT DU LOUP

107 rue de Rivoli
A1 – Louvre &
Les Halles (RB) ③
+33 (0)1 42 25 49 55
www.lesautduloup.fr

In the summertime the elegant terrace of Le Saut du Loup restaurant is the perfect place for a lunch, a drink or dinner in this privileged setting where you can feel the magic of Paris at any time of day. Enjoy the postcard views thanks to the exceptional location between the Louvre Museum and the Tuileries Gardens.

144 L'INSTITUT CULTUREL SUÉDOIS

11 rue Payenne
A3 – Marais & Bastille
(RB) ⑤
+33 (0)1 44 78 80 20
paris.si.se

The Swedish Cultural Institute is located in the historic Marais district in Hôtel de Marle. The institute organises exhibitions, concerts and film screenings. The little café at the entrance of the sun-drenched paved courtyard is an idyllic place for lunch where you can enjoy a sandwich made with the famous dark Swedish bread, enjoy a a traditional cinnamon bun at tea time or quench your thirst with some refreshing elderflower cordial.

145 LE PERCHOIR

14 rue Crespin du Gast
A11 – Belleville &
surroundings (RB) ⑨
+33 (0)1 48 06 18 48
www.leperchoir.fr

There is a panoramic terrace on the top floor of this industrial building. The ambiance in this place, which is popular with Parisian thirty-somethings, is rather relaxed. The bar, under a tent, is never empty. The snack shack serves some tapas and the large tables are perfect for chance encounters. We like this place because you can see the sun set here or talk well into the night by the light of lanterns.

144 L'INSTITUT SUÉDOIS

5

WINE BARS

---

146 CAVES LEGRAND

1 rue de la Banque
A 2 – Louvre &
Les Halles (RB) ③
+33 (0)1 42 60 07 12
www.caves-legrand.com

Step through the doors of caves Legrand and you step into history because this magnificent place has been an institution for five generations. After a quick visit of the deli sit down at the bar for a tasting, surrounded by bottles with mythical names and ask the sommelier for some assistance. The emphasis is on sharing and passing on information. That said, the discovery of some unknown wines along with some delicious snacks will only make you want to do one thing: return for more.

147 LE BARON ROUGE

1 rue Théophile
Roussel
A 12 – Marais & Bastille
(RB) ⑤
+33 (0)1 43 43 14 32

This popular wine bar, near marché d'Aligre, is very busy on Sundays towards lunch. After doing their shopping the regulars like to stand around the barrels on the pavement and enjoy dishes of oysters with a glass of white wine. The special place and the wine, which is on tap, have contributed to this place's reputation as one of the few wine bars that has retained its authenticity.

BEAUGE

148 LA CAVE DE L'INSOLITE

30 rue de la Folie
Méricourt
A 11 – Belleville &
surroundings (RB) ⑨
+33 (0)1 53 36 08 33
www.lacavedelinsolite.fr

Environmental awareness is also becoming important in the wine industry. Some establishments in Paris now offer natural and organic wines, like La cave de l'Insolite. Here the careful selection and the wide range of prices will inspire a commitment to a more environmentally-friendly agriculture. This friendly and unpretentious place is owned by two brothers who serve simple and tasty food to go with your wine.

149 LE VERRE VOLÉ

67 rue de Lancry
A 10 – Belleville &
surroundings (RB) ⑨
+33 (0)1 48 03 17 34
leverrevole.fr

This wine bar and eatery is popular among fans of vineyards that are only known by insiders, foodies and the people who live in canal Saint-Martin. The perfect place to try out wines from all the regions of France, natural wines for the most part. The wines are paired with creative dishes at reasonable prices if you consider the quality that this establishment offers.

150 LA BUVETTE

67 rue Saint-Maur
A 11 – Marais & Bastille
(RB) ⑤
+33 (0)9 83 56 94 11

This tiny bar in a former dairy with old-fashioned tiles, a few wooden tables and vintage crockery is a place of pilgrimage for fans of wines from small producers and regional products. Camille, the young owner, will advice you on the wine and prepare sandwiches with delicious country bread, cheese, terrines and other regional specialities. After 8 p.m. it can often be hard to find a place at the bar to put down your glass but this place is definitely worth a visit.

5 places
where you can buy
THE BEST SPIRITS

151 LA MAISON DU WHISKY

20 rue d'Anjou
A 8 – Arc de Triomphe,
Champs-Élysées &
Grands Boulevards
(RB) ②
+33 (0)1 42 65 03 16
www.whisky.fr

Connoisseurs and beginners who love making new discoveries all know this Parisian address very well. La Maison du Whisky was founded in 1956 by Georges Bénitah and is one of the French specialists for rare whiskeys. From a Single Malt Scotch whisky of which only one cask exists to a Breton buckwheat whiskey, this place has a vast and high-end selection worth exploring.

152 DILETTANTES

22 rue de Savoie
A 6 – Saint-Germain-
des-Prés & Mont-
parnasse (LB) ⑥
+33 (0)1 70 69 98 68
www.dilettantes.fr

If you love bubbles, then you will love discovering this champagne merchant. Check out the amazing selection of great finds from a selection of independent growers whose wines cannot be found in the supermarkets. Stop in the superb cellar where you can taste three champagnes by the glass, along with a plate of cheese or charcuterie. An excellent alternative for those who want to learn more about the various appellations.

153 PARIS ST-BIÈRE

101 rue de Charonne
A 3 – Marais & Bastille
(RB) ⑤
+33 (0)1 43 48 07 11

This is the beer temple of Paris. The shelves in these two adjoining shops are covered from floor to ceiling with a huge selection of beers from all over the world: naturally there are Belgian, French and German beers but you will also find Danish, Canadian or Italian beers here. Some are sourced from small traditional breweries, others are exclusively sold here. The very friendly owner, who is a true beer connoisseur, organises weekly tastings.

154 FINE SPIRITS

6 carrefour de l'Odéon
A 6 – Saint-Germain-
des-Prés & Mont-
parnasse (LB) ⑥
+33 (0)1 46 34 70 20
www.finespirits.fr

This large store in quartier de l'Odéon sells Fine Spirits only and has a huge selection (1,500 different spirits available). This is where aficionados go for their rum, cognac, Armagnac, vodka or other liqueurs. Mixologists will be happy to discover the amazing array of tasting and bar accessories too.

155 LA CAVE DE LA GRANDE EPICERIE DE PARIS

38 rue de Sèvres
A 7 – Saint-Germain-
des-Prés & Mont-
parnasse (LB) ⑥
+33 (0)1 44 39 81 00
*www.lagrandeepicerie.
com*

The Epicureans of Paris love this luxury food hall on the Left Bank. Its exceptional wine cellar is probably one of the reasons why they flock here. The selection is amazing: they sell 2,000 different wines, 1,000 spirits and champagnes as well as 375 exceptional vintages. You can also taste the wines on location in the bar-restaurant Balthazar and learn more about wine during the regular wine courses they organise.

5 amazing
TEA ROOMS

---

156 MAISON DES TROIS THÉS

1 rue Saint-Médard
A5 – Quartier Latin
(LB) ④
+33 (0)1 43 36 93 84
www.maisondestroisthes.com

Master Tseng is one of the greatest tea experts in the world. All the leading chefs rely on his unparalleled nose and palate. In his showroom in the Quartier Latin, where he also welcomes private individuals, he sells more than 1,000 hand-picked teas from China, Taiwan and Nepal, including several vintages. In the afternoon they teach you how to taste tea here, which is very much like savouring a fine wine. The tea cellar is perfect for learning more about this noble product.

157 MAISON GEORGE CANNON

12 rue Notre Dame des Champs
A6 – Saint-Germain-des-Prés & Montparnasse (LB) ⑥
+33 (0)1 53 63 05 43
www.georgecannon.fr

Maison George Cannon has been importing and selling tea since 1898. Their teas are widely renowned for their rich flavour and diversity. Tea connoisseurs and tea enthusiasts meet in this dainty tea house where they can choose from 250 different teas. Here they explain the subtleties of this beverage. The passionate staff will gladly teach you more about the universe and history of tea. You can have lunch here, or tea, or take part in an intimate tea ceremony.

158 JUGETSUDO

95 rue de Seine
A 6 – Saint-Germain-
des-Prés & Mont-
parnasse (LB) ⑥
+33 (0)1 46 33 94 90
www.jugetsudo.fr

Discover the art of Japanese tea and the golden rules for preparing the perfect cup of tea during the Initiation course. In this tranquil space where bamboo stalks hang from the ceiling you will be introduced to the virtues and health benefits of green tea and learn how to prepare and taste it the proper way.

159 CAFÉ VERLET

256 rue Saint-Honoré
A 1 – Louvre &
Les Halles (RB) ③
+33 (0)1 42 60 67 39
www.verlet.fr

This delightful tiny café, which is just a short walk from the Museum of Decorative Arts and the Palais Royal, is the perfect choice for a nice afternoon cuppa or a more fragrant tea. Don't forget to order the house speciality, candied fruit. Café Verlet is a popular haunt among neighbourhood locals as well anyone who appreciates a genuine place.

160 MARIAGE FRÈRES

13 rue des Grands-
Augustins
A 6 – Saint-Germain-
des-Prés & Mont-
parnasse (LB) ⑥
+33 (0)1 40 51 82 50
www.mariagefreres.com

People all over the world know this major brand and its amazing tea blends. Go to the shop in rue des Grands Augustins, which is more intimate than the others, with its adjoining tiny tea house. The 'tea walls', which were built by stacking more than 500 boxes, harbour subtle and delicate fragrances. You will also find a lot of tea accessories in this shop.

5 places for
A GOOD CUP
OF COFFEE

_____

161 LOUSTIC
40 rue Chapon
A 3 – Marais & Bastille
(RB) ⑤
+33 (0)9 80 31 07 06

This charming pocket-sized café, with its cosy, retro design, sells exceptional coffees from Kenya, Colombia and Ethiopia, which are ground on site. They also sell delicious home-made pastries, making this a good choice for breakfast or at tea time.

162 TÉLESCOPE
5 rue Villedo
A 1 – Louvre &
Les Halles (RB) ③
+33 (0)1 42 61 33 14
www.telescopecafe.com

Nicolas, the owner of Télescope, learnt the art of coffee in the United States. His charming Parisian coffee shop attracts regulars and knowledgeable tourists. He prepares filter coffee in front of his customers, serving it with a cookie and a big smile. All you need to do is enjoy your Ethiopian blend, while listening to some Nina Simone.

163 CAFÉ LOMI
3 ter Rue Marcadet
A 18 – Belleville &
surroundings (RB) ⑨
+33 (0)9 51 27 46 31
www.cafelomi.com

Café Lomi is a traditional small roastery and coffee shop that is very popular with coffee fans. This vast space, with its industrial loft-like feel, adjoining the roastery, is the place to go for an exceptional espresso or tea infusion, with a pastry or a light snack at lunch. You can also buy freshly roasted coffees here, as well as grinders, Chemex and syphons.

164 TEN BELLES

10 rue de la Grange
aux Belles
A 10 – Belleville &
surroundings (RB) ⑨
+33 (0)1 42 40 90 78
www.tenbelles.com

This café, with its laidback welcoming atmosphere takes a different approach to coffee. Purists will have their coffee without sugar so they can savour the subtle aromas while novices should rely on the advice of the baristas. The large counter is full of delicious sandwiches for lunch, which you can eat on the mezzanine, while you chat with your neighbours.

165 FONDATION CAFÉ

16 rue Dupetit-
Thouars
A 3 – Marais & Bastille
(RB) ⑤

Australian barista Christa Nielsen receives coffee lovers in this tiny coffee bar which has a decidedly Nordic feel to it. The coffee is sourced from Belleville Brûlerie, the espresso is simply perfect, balanced and aromatic. Most people end up having their coffee outside on the pavement as it can often be very crowded here.

161 LOUSTIC

EX NIHILO

60 PLACES TO SHOP

The 5 best
FLOWER SHOPS

166 ERIC CHAUVIN
22 rue Jean Nicot
A 7 – Invalides &
Eiffel Tower (LB) ⑦
+33 (0)1 45 50 43 54
www.ericchauvin.fr

This florist to the stars works for some of the biggest fashion houses like Christian Dior and has several shops all over Paris. The tiny shop in rue Jean Nicot is our favourite although it can be hard to make your way through the large displays of seasonal flowers and branches. The bouquets are natural yet refined and the staff are always on hand to provide good advice.

167 ARÔM
73 avenue Ledru-
Rollin
A 12 – Marais & Bastille
(RB) ⑤
+33 (0)1 43 46 82 59
www.aromparis.fr

Here, in this flower shop which resembles an antiques store, the staff takes the time to listen to you. After you have explained your colour preferences or have indicated your budget the florists will intuitively put together a natural yet elegant bouquet. At Arôm you need to take it slow and also listen to the florists' suggestions.

168 L'ARTISAN FLEURISTE
95 rue Vieille du
Temple
A 3 – Marais & Bastille
(RB) ⑤
+33 (0)1 42 78 40 40
www.artisanfleuriste.fr

This pretty store opposite the Piccaso Museum sells flowers of the highest quality. Bouquets and plants decorate the store's entrance, inviting you to step in and explore this shop which is teeming with beautiful species and varieties. This florist comes up with spectacular and poetic bouquets but can also suggest plants for your balcony or terrace.

169 FLOWER

14 rue des Saints-Pères
A6 – Saint-Germain-
des-Prés & Mont-
parnasse (LB) ⑥
+33 (0)1 44 50 00 20
www.flower.fr

This florist, whose shop is in the antiques
district, is known for his subtle colour combinations and the quality of the flowers he
sells. The amazing array of flowers in the
store tends to spill out onto the pavement,
lending a special charm to this place.

170 BLEUET-COQUELICOT

10 rue de la Grange
aux Belles
A10 – Belleville &
surroundings (RB) ⑨
+33 (0)1 42 41 21 35
www.bleuetcoquelicot.fr

This tiny store with its evocative name and
pretty façade is owned by Tom, a self-taught
florist who is passionate about flowers. He
sources his flowers and plants from small
local growers and takes an intuitive approach to his natural bouquets. Every plant
sold here is hand-picked by the owner, who
has managed to create a timeless atmosphere in his shop.

168 L'ARTISAN FLEURISTE

The 5 best
BOOKSHOPS

---

171 LA CHAMBRE CLAIRE
14 rue Saint-Sulpice
A 6 – ⑥
+33 (0)1 46 34 04 31
www.la-chambre-claire.fr

This tiny specialised bookshop caters to photography fans. Most of the books sold here are fine art books, sorted by theme or by photographer including some big names like Robert Doisneau, Robert Capa, Henri Cartier-Bresson and many others. They also have more technical books and a small exhibition space.

172 ARTCURIAL
7 rond-point des
Champs Élysées-
Marcel Dassault
A 8 – Arc de Triomphe,
Champs-Élysées &
Grands Boulevards
(RB) ②
+33 (0)1 42 99 20 20
www.artcurial.com

This large bookstore is located in the Artcurial auction house in the prestigious Marcel Dassault mansion and has an excellent selection of books about twentieth-century art and design as well as a wide range of books that are out of print and *catalogues raisonnés.*

173 LA LIBRAIRIE GOURMANDE
96 rue Montmartre
A 2 – Louvre &
Les Halles (RB) ③
+33 (0)1 43 54 37 27
*www.librairie
gourmande.fr*

This bookshop is dedicated to professional and amateur fans of fine cuisine. Here you can find thousands of themed books on the art of baking, wine tasting, organic food as well as cookbooks by leading chefs and even comic books.

174 CHANTELIVRE

13 rue de Sèvres
A 7 – Saint-Germain-
des-Prés & Mont-
parnasse (LB) ⑥
+33 (0)1 45 48 87 90
www.chantelivre.com

This large bookshop, which is centrally located in Saint-Germain-des-Prés, is widely renowned for its fine selection of children's books. The knowledgeable staff will gladly guide you through the thousands of books that include book/objects for babies and picture books.

175 PLAN LIBRE

122 rue de Charenton
A 12 – Marais & Bastille
(RB) ⑤
+33 (0)9 53 13 66 90
www.planlibre.com

This tiny neighbourhood bookshop is owned by someone who is 'passionate about architecture for architecture enthusiasts' and is very well-stocked. Exhibition catalogues, themed books about urban planning or landscape architecture stand alongside rare books, monographs by architects and a good selection of books about design.

The 5 best
GIFT SHOPS

---

176 DESIGN & NATURE
4 rue d'Aboukir
A 2 – Louvre &
Les Halles (RB) ③
+33 (0)1 43 06 86 98
www.designetnature.fr

This gallery, which specialises in taxidermy, sells a range of collector's items for cabinets of curiosities. Parrots, colourful butterflies, flamingos, zebras and lions all co-exist happily here in a fascinating and inspiring atmosphere. The place to go for a gift that is out of the ordinary.

177 CIRE TRUDON
78 rue de Seine
A 6 – Saint-Germain-
des-Prés & Mont-
parnasse (LB) ⑥
+33 (0)1 43 26 46 50
www.ciretrudon.com

This wax manufacturer was established in 1643 and is a must visit in Paris. The place to go for pillar candles in every possible size, bust candles of iconic figures of French history like Marie-Antoinette and the huge wall lined with candles in every possible colour, each more beautiful than the next. You'll always find a pretty gift in this paradise for candle-lovers.

178 ASTIER DE VILLATTE

173 rue Saint-Honoré
A 1 – Louvre &
Les Halles (RB) ③
+33 (0)1 42 60 74 13
www.astierdevillatte.com

The spirit of this French brand is epitomised in the amazing charm of this store. The delicate white ceramic crockery, which is inspired by models from the seventeenth and eighteenth centuries, the hand-blown glassware and home accessories are displayed in old cabinets or stacked in irregular piles. While it is true that the prices are astronomic there is simply no equivalent for this shop if it is refinement you are seeking.

179 BULY 1803

6 rue Bonaparte
A 6 – Saint-Germain-
des-Prés & Mont-
parnasse (LB) ⑥
+33 (0)1 43 29 02 50
www.buly1803.com

The founders of this shop with its astounding interior had the brilliant idea to reopen a shop selling products created by the famous perfumer Buly since 1803. They sell virgin oils for various skin or hair concerns, incense manufactured by the monks of Mount Athos in Greece and beauty accessories from all over the world, including a sandalwood comb or volcanic pumice stones. This dainty shop is the perfect place to buy yourself an exceptional gift.

180 KHADI AND CO

82 boulevard
Beaumarchais
A 11 – Marais & Bastille
(RB) ⑤
+33 (0)1 43 57 10 25
www.khadiandco.com

Khadi and Co is the combination of Indian textile expertise with the talent of the Danish designer, Bess Nielsen. These elegant and durable hand-woven cotton, silk and wool products, including bed linens, tablecloths, stoles and kurta shirts are a real homage to the rigorous and functional Scandinavian tradition and the subtle and refined Indian workmanship.

The 5 best places for
GRAPHIC ART AND PAPER

181 PAPIER+

9 rue du Pont Louis-
Philippe
A4 – Marais & Bastille
(RB) ⑤
+33 (0)1 42 77 70 49
www.papierplus.com

This pretty stationery shop is known for its amazing notebooks, which are called *livres blancs* (white books) and come in various sizes. They are locally made by craftsman who employ traditional expertise to make them. The range of colours is subtle and varied, which explains why these notebooks are so popular. PAPIER+ also sells a wide range of gift sets, binders and photo albums.

182 PAPIER TIGRE

5 rue des Filles du
Calvaire
A3 – Marais & Bastille
(RB) ⑤
+33 (0)1 48 04 00 21
www.papiertigre.fr

This tiny brand has energised the French stationery industry with its range of notebooks, calendars and greeting cards made of colourful recycled paper with graphic designs. Papier Tigre designs, manufactures and distributes fun objects for daily use in a contemporary Parisian spirit.

183 ADELINE KLAM

54 boulevard Richard Lenoir
A11 – Marais & Bastille
(RB) ⑤
+33 (0)1 48 07 20 88
www.adelineklam.com

Adeline loves patterns and colours and sells a wide range of Japanese paper in her bright and airy shop. The paper, which is made of long mulberry fibres, is ideal for paper creations, book binding, origami and decorative purposes. The owner will gladly tell you more about which paper to use for your creations.

184 CALLIGRANE

6 rue du Pont Louis-Philippe
A4 – Marais & Bastille
(RB) ⑤
+33 (0)1 48 04 09 00
www.calligrane.fr

Since 1979 this shop has been specialising in fine art papers selling rare paper from Japan, vegetable-based sheets, exceptional products like sequoia wood envelopes as well as limited editions of art works. This is the perfect shop for purists and people who love stunning materials.

185 LA PETITE PAPETERIE FRANÇAISE

FOR SALE AT
PALAIS DE TOKYO
13 avenue du Président Wilson
A16 – Arc de Triomphe, Champs-Élysées & Grands Boulevards (RB) ②
+33 (0)1 49 52 02 04
www.lapetitepapeterie francaise.fr
www.palaisdetokyo.com

This small brand, which was established by Sylvie Bétard, who is passionate about anything 'made in France' sells beautiful environment-friendly products, catering to all stationery fans who also care about the environment. The notebooks, the stationery and the envelopes are made with care by printers who are truly artisans. This exceptional stationery is sold in the bookstore of Palais de Tokyo and through the brand's website.

The 5 best
MADE-TO-MEASURE BOUTIQUES

---

186 LA CERISE SUR LE CHAPEAU

11 rue Cassette
A6 – Saint-Germain-
des-Prés & Mont-
parnasse (LB) ⑥
+33 (0)1 45 49 90 53
*www.
lacerisesurlechapeau.com*

In this (work)shop you can choose the shape, the ribbon and the colour of your hat. A felt hat for winter or a straw hat for summer, panama or poplin, simple or flashy colours… there is something for everyone. On weekdays they take about an hour to make you a hat, just enough time for a stroll around the neighbourhood.

187 JLR

28 rue Saint-Sulpice
A6 – Saint-Germain-
des-Prés & Mont-
parnasse (LB) ⑥
+33 (0)1 40 46 06 77
www.jlrparis.com

This shop is the perfect place to find a gift for the man in your life. Choose a shirt, the shape of the collar, the colour or pattern, a traditional shirt or a something more modern. Finally, as the height of luxury, have his initials embroidered on the shirt in the font of your choice. And you can even buy matching underwear!

188 LIN & CIE

16 rue Bréa
A6 – Saint-Germain-
des-Prés & Mont-
parnasse (LB) ⑥
+33 (0)1 43 54 43 32
*www.linetcompagnie.
blogs.com*

This tiny shop is ideally suited if you're looking for a customised gift for a newborn. You can have the baby's name embroidered on all kinds of objects made of linen, poplin or Liberty fabric including toiletry bags, cushions, satchels and onesies. What's more you can even add a fun illustration like a Vespa or a guitar.

189 **AU FIL DES LETTRES**

34 rue Michel-Ange
A 16
+33 (0)1 42 24 44 49
www.aufildeslettres.com

Marie-Brune de Dreux-Brézé and Béatrice Hintzy are the queens of personalised gifts. You can develop the most refined gifts and the most inconceivable ideas with them, whether you're thinking of embroidered napkins for a special dinner, an engraved crystal paperweight or a customised seat for your child. At Au Fil des Lettres they take the time to choose the gift that is best suited to the occasion.

190 **EX NIHILO**

352 rue Saint-Honoré
A 1 – Arc de Triomphe, Champs-Élysées & Grands Boulevards
(RB) ②
www.ex-nihilo-paris.com

This magnificent perfumery sells eight exclusive fragrances that have been created by eight of the best 'noses' in the world. After having chosen your favourite you can add a personal touch to it to make it even more sublime. May rose, jasmine, vanilla… Choose from three different scents for each fragrance. The store's accommodating staff will help you make a selection.

190 EX NIHILO

The 5 best
HOME DECORATION SHOPS

---

191 CARAVANE

19 & 22 rue Saint-Nicolas
A 12 – Marais & Bastille
(RB) ⑤
+33 (0)1 43 40 79 66
www.caravane.fr

Any Parisian woman with a penchant for home decoration knows these two shops. They pay great attention to the quality of the fabrics, the prints and the colours. Their selection of bed linens, curtains and crockery is subtle, refined and eclectic as they are inspired by India, Morocco and Asia.

192 MERCI

111 boulevard Beaumarchais
A 3 – Marais & Bastille
(RB) ⑤
+33 (0)1 42 77 00 33
www.merci-merci.com

Since its opening in 2009 this unique concept store is a must see on any shopping spree in Paris, especially its magnificent furniture, home accessories and tableware departments. The international selection, which combines contemporary designs, unique and vintage pieces, always has a surprise in store for you.

193 SIMRANE

25 rue Bonaparte
A 6 – Saint-Germain-des-Prés & Montparnasse (LB) ⑥
+33 (0)1 43 54 90 73
www.simrane.com

This place is not that well known but it has the best selection of Indian fabrics in Paris. The block painting patterns on the shop's sarongs, bedspreads, cushions, tablecloths and kimonos, are especially amazing. In fact the combinations of colours and patterns are so stunning that choosing can be quite agonising.

195 **LA TRÉSORERIE**

194 **ULRIKE WEISS**

194 ULRIKE-WEISS

12 passage des
Taillandiers
A11 – Marais & Bastille
(RB) ⑤
+33 (0)9 50 23 24 47
www.ulrike-weiss.com

The ceramist Ulrike Weiss sells her delicate porcelain creations and glazed lava tiles in her charming workshop/store in *Quartier de la Bastille*. These visually stunning and poetic objects for daily use have a rather Nordic look and feel to them and the range of colours and textures is very nice too. All the artist's creations are exclusively sold here.

195 LA TRÉSORERIE

11 rue du Château
d'eau
A 10 – Belleville &
surroundings (RB) ⑨
+33 (0)1 40 40 20 46
latresorerie.fr

La Trésorerie is very similar to the old emporiums where you could buy anything you needed for a 'well-kept' house. Under the glass roof you can find pretty, useful and environmentally-friendly items including a nice selection of homewares, industrial stools, table linens as well as organic paint and cleaning products.

The 5 best
CONTEMPORARY DESIGN SHOPS

---

196 FR 66

25 rue du Renard
A 4 – Louvre &
Les Halles (RB) ③
+33 (0)1 44 54 35 36
www.fr66.com

The two sisters who founded this shop have put together one of the most sophisticated selections of objects and furniture in Paris. They love minimalist and radical designs and work with established and up-and-coming designers. They are also excellent advisers when it comes to restyling your interior, down to the smallest details.

197 COLONEL

14 avenue Richerand
A 10 – Belleville &
surroundings (RB) ⑨
+33 (0)1 83 89 69 22
www.moncolonel.fr

Colonel sells a vibrant and contemporary selection of items, with a mix of pretty colours and timeless designs. The light fixtures designed by the two owners of the store and the Scandinavian furniture by some of the best brands in the market are the highlights of this beautiful shop.

198 MARCEL BY BOUTIQUE

28 rue Saint-Claude
A 3 – Marais & Bastille
(RB) ⑤
+33 (0)1 57 40 80 77
www.marcelby.fr

This shop has the perfect Marais location and presents a hard to resist selection of trendy brands, independent labels and designers. Here you find practical but at the same time poetic everyday objects like glassware by Laurence Brabant or furniture pieces made by talented contemporary designers.

199 GALLERY S. BENSIMON

111 rue de Turenne
A3 – Marais & Bastille
(RB) ⑤
+33 (0)1 42 74 50 77
www.gallerybensimon.
com

Gallery S. Bensimon wants to give contemporary designers the freedom to express themselves in this space. The gallery was founded by the fashion designer Serge Bensimon. He has a knack for discovering talented artists and likes to find upcoming young designers. The gallery regularly hosts themed exhibitions where you can always find something unique.

200 THE COLLECTION

33 rue de Poitou
A3 – Marais & Bastille
(RB) ⑤
+33 (0)1 42 77 04 20
www.thecollection.fr

Allison Grant, who originally hails from Britain, opened her store The Collection in le Marais, selling an amazing collection of wallpapers. Some of these are works of art in their own right, like the embroidered designs, or the gilded ones with gilt leaf. Others create an illusion like the trompe-l'oeil wallpapers, the patterned and 3D wallpapers.

197 COLONEL

The 5 best
VINIninTAGE DESIGN SHOPS

---

201 MAISON NORDIK
159 rue Marcadet
A 18 – Montmartre
(RB) ⑧
+33 (0)6 22 07 21 07
maisonnordik.com

This large store, which is off the beaten track on *la butte* Montmartre sells one of the best selections of Scandinavian furniture in Paris. Here you will find all kinds of classics including teak sideboards, ceramic vases, light fixtures by Poul Henningsen as well as a wide range of furniture and objects with simple designs in quality materials. If you feel pangs of nostalgia when thinking about the Fifties and Sixties then you need to visit this shop.

202 LES MODERNISTES
3 avenue du Père-Lachaise
A 20 – Belleville & surroundings (RB) ⑨
+33 (0)6 26 12 37 41
lesmodernistesparis. blogspot.be

This gallery, which is located near the entrance of Père-Lachaise, is widely considered an expert in design of the Fifties, Sixties and Seventies. Expect a mix of furniture, objects, sculptures and painters by anonymous designers with signed designs. The gallery also sells a nice selection of contemporary jewellery and pottery.

203 CHRISTINE DIEGONI
47 ter rue d'Orsel
A 18 – Montmartre
(RB) ⑧
+33 (0)1 42 64 69 48
www.christinediegoni.fr

Design collectors have already found their way to this shop in Montmartre which sells exceptional items and furniture by leading designers such as Ettore Sottsass or George Nelson. The light fixtures by the Italian designer Gino Sarfatti, in which Christine Diegoni specialises, are the highlight of this shop.

204 **ATELIER 154**

14/16 rue Neuve
Popincourt
A 11 – Belleville &
surroundings (RB) ⑨
+33 (0)6 62 32 79 06
www.atelier154.com

Stéphane Quatresous initially specialised
in industrial design but then became interested in Dutch design from the Fifties. In
this large store, which resembles a design
studio, you can find an interesting mix of
office furniture and industrial light fixtures
with Friso Kramer's sleek chairs or the
pared down designs of Wim Rietvelt. There
are some excellent discoveries to be made
here.

205 **FORME UTILE**

5 passage Charles
Dallery
A 11 – Marais & Bastille
(RB) ⑤
+32 (0)1 43 55 26 07
www.formeutile.com

Richard Poulet chose to name his store after a post-war French movement, as an ode
to industrial design. He specialises in light
fixtures and furniture and works much
like a historian, searching, unearthing
and finding items. Shop here for work by
leading designers from the Fifties as well as
lesser known designers who may become
the stars of tomorrow's auctions.

201 MAISON NORDIK

The 5 most charming
ANTIQUE SHOPS

206 VERREGLASS

32 rue de Charonne
A11 – Marais & Bastille
(RB) ⑤
+33 (0)1 48 05 78 43

This discreet store is full of vases and glassware of all sizes and colours. Claudius Breig likes to unearth Italian, Scandinavian and French glassware from the 19th century to the Seventies. He can advise you about a purchase and is passionate about every item he sells. Here you will only find originals, no trends or fads.

207 BAC ANTIQUITÉS

122 rue du Bac
A 7 – Saint-Germain-des-Prés & Mont-parnasse (LB) ⑥
+33 (0)1 45 44 87 39

This store stands out in this street which is full of high-end brands. The disorder is incredible but the charismatic owner somehow manages to keep it all under control, selling huge decorative plane components (propellers, engines, air intakes). If you are looking for a candleholder, Scandinavian ceramics or pretty silver-plated dishes then this is also a good place to start.

208 BELLE LURETTE

5 rue du Marché Popincourt
A 11 – Belleville & surroundings (RB) ⑨
+33 (0)1 43 38 67 39

This store is the largest in this charming housing block where you can find a lot of second-hand furniture shops and trendy eateries. The eclectic mix of restored home furniture, charming objects, Seventies chairs, light fixtures in a variety of styles and homewares, makes this the perfect place to add some soul to your interior at an affordable price.

209 AU PETIT BONHEUR LA CHANCE

13 rue Saint-Paul
A4 – Marais & Bastille
(RB) ⑤
+33 (0)1 42 74 36 38

This tiny store in village Saint-Paul is nostalgia central as this is where the owner stores all our childhood memories. Breakfast china, school notebooks, piles of old cloths, haberdashery items, books... The place to go for Parisians and tourists who love vintage decoration.

210 MARION HELD JAVAL

66 rue Lhomond
A5 – Saint-Germain-
des-Prés & Mont-
parnasse (LB) ⑥
+33 (0)6 80 66 23 61
www.marionheld
javal.com

The antiques dealer Marion Held Javal opens her very tastefully appointed house every first Friday of the month to the public, from 11 am until 7 pm. Each time she puts together an amazing selection of decorative objects and curiosities, old posters and twentieth-century design. This exclusive, visually stunning gallery is truly worth the detour if you happen to be in Paris.

The 5 best
STREET MARKETS
in Paris

211 LA BROCANTE DE LA RUE DE BRETAGNE

Rue de Bretagne & rue de Belleyme, rue de Turenne, the area around Carreau du Temple, rue Dupetit Thouars, adjoining streets
A3 – Marais & Bastille
(RB) ⑤

Twice a year professionals and private individuals gather for three days of flea market fun in the centre of le Marais. This large market mainly focuses on furniture and clothes from the Fifties, Sixties and Seventies. The market attracts hipsters, families and people strolling through and is eagerly awaited. It is such a success that the prices continue to soar year after year.

212 LES PUCES DU DESIGN

Bercy Village
28 rue François Truffaut
A12 – Marais & Bastille
(RB) ⑤
www.pucesdudesign.com

This street market only sells design from the Fifties to the Noughties. It is unique in France in that it gathers all the top vendors in this niche who set aside their best pieces for the occasion. Whether you just like to look or are searching for a unique piece of furniture by your favourite designer, this street market is a must. There is also always an exhibition about a leading designer.

213 LA BROCANTE DE L'AVENUE DE TRUDAINE

Avenue de Trudaine
A 9 – Montmartre
(RB) ⑧

Twice a year this neighbourhood street market occupies one of the prettiest avenues in Paris. Although you will preponderantly find industrial furniture and Seventies design here there are also more traditional stalls that sell an eclectic mix of items in different styles and from different eras. The best time to visit is in the early morning when the sellers are setting up shop and the surrounding cafes start to serve breakfast.

214 PUCES DE VANVES

Avenue Marc
Sangnier, avenue
Georges Lafenestre
A 14 – Invalides &
Eiffel Tower (LB) ⑦

This street market, which is just outside of the city centre, gathers more than 300 antiques dealers. The atmosphere is genuine and friendly. Here you can find anything from old photos and postcards to garden furniture and curiosities. Come early if you're looking for that rare gem.

215 LA FOIRE DE CHATOU

Île des
Impressionnistes
Chatou
www.foiredechatou.com

This major fair is organised twice a year for twelve days in Île des Impressionists in Chatou, just 10 minutes outside of Paris. Hundreds of antiques dealers from all over France present their best finds here. It is also known as the *foire aux jambons* (ham fair) as part of the exhibition space is dedicated to some of the best regional produce. Stroll through the aisles and enjoy the people watching.

The 5 most interesting
STALLS AT LES PUCES DE SAINT-OUEN

216 LIBRAIRIE DE L'AVENUE

Marché aux Puces
31 rue Lécuyer
Saint-Ouen –
Montmartre (RB) ⑧
+33 (0)1 40 11 95 85
www.librairie-avenue.com

This bookstore is located in the heart of the street market and is the largest second-hand book store in the Parisian region. Here you can find all sorts of books, including pockets and fine books, old journals and collector's items, in every possible domain. The unique atmosphere of this huge bookstore makes it a must visit if you're going to the street market.

217 CHEZ SARAH

18 rue Jules Vallès
Saint-Ouen –
Montmartre (RB) ⑧
+33 (0)6 08 01 80 89
www.chezsarah.net

Sarah Rozenbaum is the third generation of her family with a stall in this street market, following in her mother's and grandmother's footsteps. She is passionate about fashion and couture and is considered an expert in the style of the Twenties, Thirties, Forties and Fifties. Sarah also advises young women as they search for a wedding dress.

218 MARCHÉ L'USINE

18 rue des Bons Enfants
Saint-Ouen –
Montmartre (RB) ⑧

This immense warehouse, which resembles a market, is not as busy and not as popular as its neighbours Paul Bert or Serpette. But we recommend venturing there because you will enjoy finding rare gems or unusual items here even it means your hands will get a little dirty.

219 LA MARELLE

Marché Dauphine,
Stand 86
132-140 rue des
Rosiers
Saint-Ouen –
Montmartre (RB) ⑧

Catherine Lambert is passionate about children's furniture, scouring street markets and restoring timeless and original items. This pretty store sells desks, wooden toys, prints from the Thirties, tiny chairs by leading designers, garden furniture and anecdotal objects and is sure to appeal to both the young and their parents.

220 QUINTESSENCE PLAYGROUND

3 rue Paul Bert
Saint-Ouen –
Montmartre (RB) ⑧
+33 (0)6 18 99 18 25

This elegant two-floor concept store, devised by Ludovic Messager, sells extravagant items, industrial furniture, curiosities and even whole interiors which you can transpose to your home. His taste and his flair for interior decoration appeal to a rich clientele because all the stars shop at Quintessence Playground.

The 5 places to go for
KITCHENWARE

221 COURTY & FILS
44 rue des Petits
Champs
A 2 – Louvre &
Les Halles (RB) ③
+33 (0)1 42 96 59 21
www.couteaux-courty.com

Courty sells genuine handcrafted knives, from factories all over France including original creations by reputable French artisans as well as traditional Japanese and Finnish knives. Need a potato peeler or a Swiss knife, then visit the Parisian kingdom of the knife.

222 MORA
13 rue Montmartre
A 1 – Louvre &
Les Halles (RB) ③
+33 (0)1 45 08 19 24
www.mora.fr

All the leading chefs and pastry chefs worldwide use Mora utensils. If you want to follow their example then head over to this cave of Ali Baba where you will find all the paraphernalia you can think of: cookware, moulds, kitchen machines as well as the tools you need for some stunning cake decorations.

223 CULINARION
99 rue de Rennes
A 6 – Saint-Germain-
des-Prés & Mont-
parnasse (LB) ⑥
+33 (0)1 45 48 94 76
www.culinarion.com

This store sells absolutely everything you need to cook, from the preparation stage to the actual meal itself. Culinarion's displays include a wide range of indispensable and fun kitchen accessories. Whether you are looking for a simple preserving pan, a siphon or a cooking thermometer they have it all.

224 LE CREUSET

51 rue de Rennes
A 6 – Saint-Germain-
des-Prés & Mont-
parnasse (LB) ⑥
+33 (0)9 64 11 55 56
www.lecreuset.fr

Le Creuset has specialised in cast iron pots since 1925. In its Parisian store the brand offers a wide range of models in various sizes and colours as well as its porcelain enamelled cast iron cookware of impeccable quality, which have contributed to the brand's success.

225 LA BOVIDA

36 rue Montmartre
A 1 – Louvre &
Les Halles (RB) ③
+33 (0)1 42 36 09 99
www.labovida.com

This beautiful store, which is a favourite of epicureans and food lovers, has everything you need to cook: kitchenware, equipment, spices from all over the world and special ingredients. The selection of books which includes bestsellers and books on a variety of original themes is also worth the visit.

KILOSHOP

35 PLACES
FOR FASHION

Comourelin - charm bracelet - making
charm since 1880   39 Rue des Francs-
www.bijoux commourelin.com   Bourgeois

226 MARIE-HÉLÈNE DE TAILLAC

8 rue de Tournon
A 6 – Saint-Germain-
des-Prés & Mont-
parnasse (LB) ⑥
+33 (0)1 44 27 07 07
*www.mariehelene
detaillac.com*

For her Parisian outlet this amazing designer worked with the British designer Tom Dixon. The powder blue walls, the poppy red furniture and the mirrors only highlight her unique designs with coloured gems from all over the world. Marie-Helène de Taillac's jewellery is very popular because of its refinement and the vibrant designs.

227 AIMÉE.AIMER

28 rue Notre-Dame
des Victoires
A 2 – Louvre &
Les Halles (RB) ③
+33 (0)1 44 54 52 00
(sur rendez-vous)
www.aimee-aimer.com

The two designers of this elegant and colourful jewellery design brand create Parisian designs with a Brazilian spirit. Their store on the first floor is welcoming and intimate, because buying jewellery is never a trivial matter. The designers are at your disposal, in their airy and calm shop, where the various collections are on display.

228 MEDECINE DOUCE

10 rue de Marseille
A 10 – Belleville &
surroundings (RB) ⑨
+33 (0)1 82 83 11 53
*www.bijouxmedecine
douce.com*

In this studio/shop near canal Saint-Martin the designer Marie Montaud designs and manufactures her delicate jewels with a bohemian spirit. The necklaces and bracelets with quirky details which mix various unexpected materials have contributed to the success of this small Parisian brand.

229 **DELPHINE PARIENTE**

101 rue de Turenne
A3 – Marais & Bastille
(RB) ⑤
+33 (0)1 42 71 84 64
www.delphinepariente.fr

Delphine Pariente gives old jewellery a second life. Starting from mismatched earrings or a family heirloom the designer creates something new, tapping into her treasure chest of vintage items. Delphine has also developed a customisable range of jewellery including bracelets, rings and medallions in gold or silver on which you can have a word or phrase of your choice inscribed.

230 **MARION VIDAL**

13 avenue Trudaine
A9 – Montmartre
(RB) ⑧
+33 (0)1 49 24 04 01
www.marionvidal.com

Marion Vidal trained as an architect, retaining a clear sense of structure and volume. She creates sculptural jewellery, which is both majestic and graphic and likes to mix materials. Her statement pieces add a certain *je ne sais quoi* to any outfit.

www. denaive : com
Dominique Denave - resin
7 rue du 29 Juillet (close to louvre)

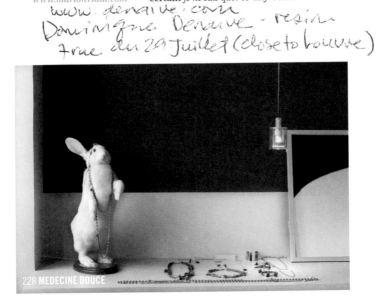

228 MEDECINE DOUCE

The 5 most innovative
CONCEPTS-STORES

---

231 THE BROKEN ARM

12 rue Perrée
A 3 – Marais & Bastille
(RB) ⑤
+33 (0)1 44 61 53 60
www.the-broken-arm.com

This store sells a nice selection of designer clothing for men and women, as well as leather goods and art books. The adjacent café, which is very popular with the trendy young people in the neighbourhood, has a soothing and minimalist interior, compensating for the shop's somewhat snobbish atmosphere.

232 FRENCH TROTTERS

30 rue de Charonne
A 4 – Marais & Bastille
(RB) ⑤
+33 (0)1 47 00 84 35
www.frenchtrotters.fr

Carole and Clarent launched their own brand ten years ago, driven by the same passion for travel, art and fashion. Theirs is a chic, minimalist and laidback aesthetic. The shop sells an exclusive selection of French, American and Japanese items.

233 SPREE

16 rue la Vieuville
A 18 – Montmartre
(RB) ⑧
+33 (0)1 42 23 41 40
www.spree.fr

The stylist Roberta Oprandi and the artist Bruno Hadjadj opened this new-style store/gallery in Montmartre where they sell a mix of items by designers from the Fifties and contemporary artists. Clothes, furniture, accessories or works of art… Every season you can discover new talent here.

Goyard – bags 233 rue saint-
Honoré
www. goyard. com

234 SOWEARE

40 rue de Charonne
A11 – Marais & Bastille
(RB) ⑤
+33 (0)9 82 37 63 91
www.soweare-shop.fr

This concept store, which was opened by two friends, Magali and Hélène, sells an eclectic mix of ready to wear items, as well as small decorative items, jewellery and other treats which they picked up in France, the UK and Scandinavia. They like colour and prints. The perfect place if you are looking for a small or large gift because they have items in a wide range of prices.

235 CENTRE COMMERCIAL

2 rue de Marseille
A 10 – Belleville &
surroundings (RB) ⑨
+33 (0)1 42 02 26 08
www.centrecommercial.cc

This high-end store near canal Saint-Martin sells the products and works of designers, craftsmen and artists with a local and environment-friendly dimension. You can find clothes here as well as second-hand bicycles, old furniture and books.

235 CENTRE COMMERCIAL

The 5 best

SECOND-HAND CLOTHES SHOPS

─────────

236 KILO SHOP

69-71 rue de la Verrerie
A4 – Marais & Bastille
(RB) ⑤
+33 (0)9 67 13 79 54
www.kilo-shop.fr

The concept of this store, which also has sister stores in Amsterdam, Athens and Tokyo, is pretty original: you can buy second-hand clothes by the kilo here. Twenty euros for a kilo of denim or 30 euros for the same weight in fur. Hats, leather trousers or vintage dresses… you will always find something to your liking in this large Parisian boutique.

237 RAG

81 rue Saint-Honoré
A1 – Louvre &
Les Halles (RB) ③
+33 (0)1 40 28 48 44

This second-hand clothes store is a favourite haunt of Parisian stylists and offers vintage designer clothes with prices ranging between 20 and 1,000 euros. No digging around here. All the clothes are nicely labelled and displayed. The store has a magnificent shoe collection too.

238 LA JOLIE GARDE-ROBE

15 rue Commines
A4 – Marais & Bastille
(RB) ⑤
+33 (0)1 42 72 13 90

Go to this chic second-hand clothes store if you are looking for a cheap Haute Couture treasure. The clothes, which range from the Twenties to the Nineties, are hand-picked. The owner looks for rare items, with character, or a certain refinement. This pretty shop is different from others because of the mint condition of these vintage items and the unique atmosphere. They only sell women's clothes and many a stylist goes hunting for special items here.

239 TILT VINTAGE

16 rue Saint-Placide
A6 – Saint-Germain-
des-Prés & Mont-
parnasse (LB) ⑥
+33 (0)9 67 07 58 86
www.tilt-vintage.com

This store is one of the rare second-hand clothes stores on the Left Bank. It sells a large range of clothes in good condition, from the Sixties to the Nineties. The prices are reasonable: between 25 and 30 euros for shoes, 20 euros for a dress or 15 euros for a *chemise (*shirt). One of the pluses is that the clothes are rigorously ordered in the shop.

240 FREE'P'STAR

20 rue de Rivoli
A4 – Marais & Bastille
(RB) ⑤
+33 (0)1 42 77 63 43
www.freepstar.com

The place to go for real second-hand clothes store fans. Free'P'Star has three stores in the heart of le Marais and is a Parisian institution. Here you can find old items as well as more recent items. Come on Monday and Tuesday, when new items arrive. The prices are very affordable and the atmosphere truly amazing.

handwritten: BHV (like Macy's) 55 rue de la Verrière

The 5 best

FASHION SHOPS
FOR WOMEN

handwritten: Parapluies Simon - umbrellas 56 blvd Saint-Michel

241 EROTOKRITOS

109 boulevard
Beaumarchais
A3 – Marais & Bastille
(RB) ⑤
+33 (0)1 42 78 14 04
www.erotokritos.com

This Cypriot designer, who has relocated to Paris, designs vibrant and colourful collections. His clothes follow the latest trends but he likes to add an original detail or cut. The tiny boutique which is tucked away in a small courtyard off boulevard Beaumarchais has plenty of lovely day dresses, tunics and trousers.

242 SŒUR

88 rue Bonaparte
A6 – Saint-Germain-
des-Prés & Mont-
parnasse (LB) ⑥
+33 (0)1 46 34 19 33
www.soeur-online.fr

Sœur is the brainchild of Domitille and Angélique Brion and caters to young women between the ages of 10 and 18 years, who are not quite a girl, not yet a woman. Their designs strike a perfect balance between childhood and adulthood and include a line of chic and timeless basics in soft hues. For once mums will be stealing clothes from their daughters' wardrobes and not the other way around.

243 ANDREA CREWS

83 rue de Turenne
A3 – Marais & Bastille
(RB) ⑤
+33 (0)1 45 26 36 68
www.andreacrews.com

The store of the artists' collective Andrea Crews is the perfect place to go if you need some *joie de vivre* to cheer you up. This kingdom of eccentricity sells madcap designs with crazy patterns in flashy colours. The brand is a pioneer in terms of upcycling and likes to overturn the conventions of fashion with clothes made of second-hand clothes.

*[handwritten: www. Noriem - crinkle fabric coats
Noriem.fr   27 Rue Vielle - du
Temple (Marais)]*

244 MAISON STANDARDS

12 place de la Bastille
Cour Damoye
A11 – Marais & Bastille
(RB) ⑤
www.maisonstandards.
com

This boutique presents a selection of time-less and clean-cut clothing pieces in subtle colours. Silk or jeans shirts, cashmere sweaters, cotton sweats, woolen stoles: this place is all about everyday essentials. The boutique-cum-showroom is located in a beautiful alley nearby the Bastille square and is the perfect place to stock up on reasonably priced basics.

245 SÉZANE

1 rue Saint-Fiacre
A2 – Louvre &
Les Halles (RB) ③
www.sezane.com

The clothes and accessories that Morgane Sézalory designs are feminine, poetic and Parisian. She has a great eye for detail, she knows how to make clothes comfortable and she senses what's hot and happening: that's why her sophisticated designs are perfect for a day in the city as well as for a night out. The designer hosts 'Happy Shop-ping' days on a regular basis and sometimes invites her clients to visit the ground floor of her studio, called 'l'appartement'. You have to register online on her website.

243 ANDREA CREWS

The 5 best
VINTAGE CLOTHING
SHOPS

---

246 RAGTIME

23 rue de l'Echaudé
A6 – Saint-Germain-
des-Prés & Mont-
parnasse (LB) ⑥
+33 (0)9 52 570 036

Françoise Auguet, the owner, is an expert in haute couture from the nineteenth and twentieth centuries, making her expertise and discerning eye available to her clientele of regulars, selling a selection by some of the finest designers. This place is a must visit for vintage fashion in Paris.

247 DIDIER LUDOT

24 galerie de
Montpensier
A1 – Louvre &
Les Halles (RB) ③
+33 (0)1 42 96 06 56
www.didierludot.fr

Didier Ludot is a pioneer. He opened his shop, which is devoted vintage couture in the gardens of Palais-Royal in 1975. Dresses, bags, shoes, jewellery… he only sells iconic pieces by some of the finest houses like Chanel, Yves Saint-Laurent, Courrèges and Hermès. He has a devoted international clientele which travels from far away to this temple of Parisian chic.

248 MAMIE BLUE

69 rue de
Rochechouart
A9 – Montmartre
(RB) ⑧
+33 (0)1 42 81 10 42
www.mamie-vintage.com

Ultra stylish Brigitte will welcome you with a smile in her rock and roll universe, which has a heavy Fifties feel to it. Find what you need for any occasion, whether a wedding or an evening out in this two-storey shop. Or maybe you are searching for an original accessory? This place is a real goldmine of glasses, belts, dresses, hats, coats and even golf trousers!

249 MADEMOISELLE STEINITZ

77 rue des Rosiers
Saint-Ouen
www.mademoiselle
steinitz.com

This vintage-boutique-cum-curiosity-cabinet is the place to be if you're looking for a specific selection of clothing by famous couturiers mixed with contemporary art pieces and old furniture, presented in a surprising and personal set-up.

250 FALBALA

PUCES DE SAINT-OUEN
MARCHÉ DAUPHINE,
STAND 284-285:
140 rue des Rosiers
Saint-Ouen
Montmartre (RB) ⑧
+33 (0)6 89 15 83 82

Françoise and Erwan Fligué have been running a stall in Marché Dauphine in the Saint-Ouen street market since 2000 and are considered the reference in terms of really old clothes. They even serve their customers in costume! Their two stalls, one for women and one for men, are frequented by the cream of the crop of costumers and are teeming with lace, accessories, bags and clothes from the 18th century to the Eighties.

247 **DIDIER LUDOT**

The 5 best
FASHION SHOPS
FOR MEN

251 KITSUNÉ

10 rue de Richelieu
A 1 – Louvre &
Les Halles (RB) ③
+33 (0)1 42 60 34 28
www.kitsune.fr

Gildas Loaec, who hails from Brittany, and Japanese Masaya Kurori opened Kitsuné in 2002. This concept store combines music with fashion. Since then their brand has become a reference: they produce the music of promising artists as well as creating the type of clothes that no self-respecting Parisian hipster can live without.

252 DOURSOUX

3 passage Alexandre
A 15 – Invalides &
Eiffel Tower (LB) ⑦
+33 (0)1 43 27 00 97
doursoux.com

This warehouse is chock-full of military jackets, Fifties trousers which were worn by the French Air Force and helmets for Mirage pilots. You will find everything you need for a costume party or a trek in the most extreme conditions at this army surplus store.

253 ISHOES

26 rue du Roi de Sicile
A 4 – Marais & Bastille
(RB) ⑤
+33 (0)1 48 04 00 30
www.ishoes.fr

This store, which is located in the heart of le Marais, specialises in vintage trainers or sneakers as Americans call them and is popular with collectors. It sells iconic models of the sportswear movement like vintage Nike Blazers or Authentic Vans as well as Reebok pumps, Nike Air Vortex or Adidas Gazelles.

254 CHARVET

28 place Vendôme
A1 – Arc de Triomphe,
Champs-Élysées &
Grands Boulevards
(RB) ②
+33 (0)1 42 60 30 70

This mythical shirt maker is only a short walk from place Vendôme and is also the place to buy high-end ties. They sell thousands of different models, in a myriad of colours, with elegant patterns in a variety of styles. The place to go for future grooms but also CEOs and movie stars.

255 MONSIEUR LACENAIRE

57 rue Charlot
A3 – Marais & Bastille
(RB) ⑤
+33 (0)1 42 77 36 04
www.monsieurlacenaire.
com

Garance Broca, the designer of this brand which specialises in knitwear, learnt the tricks of the trade at Hermès and Balmain where she developed a taste for high quality fabrics and elegant and stylish cuts. The knitted alpaca varsity sweater is the signature piece of this Marais-based shop but you can also buy cardigans, shirts, trousers with funky patterns and subtle details here.

The five best
HABERDASHERIES
in Paris

---

256 LA MERCERIE DE CHARONNE

69 rue de Charonne
A 11 – Marais & Bastille
(RB) ⑤
+33 (0)1 43 55 31 46
*www.mercerie
decharonne.fr*

This neighbourhood haberdashery with its fuchsia pink store front is definitely one of the cheapest in Paris. The friendly owner sells her wares to fashion students, upholstery shops in the neighbourhood as well as designers and amateur dressmakers. They all flock here because of the amazing selection of buttons, needles, lace, ribbons, patterns and sundries.

257 LA CROIX & LA MANIÈRE

36 rue Faidherbe
A 11 – Marais & Bastille
(RB) ⑤
+33 (0)1 43 72 99 09
*www.lacroixet
lamaniere.com*

Embroidery fans love to shop in this dainty shop. The displays are exquisite. The buttons are stored in jars while the rolls of fabrics and the spools of ribbons are sorted by colour. Here you can find colourful yarns, scissors for pros, specialised books as well as some good advice from the owners who, it's fair to say, have a monopoly on good taste when it comes to embroidery.

258 DAM BOUTONS

46 rue d'Orsel
A 18 – Montmartre
(RB) ⑧
+33 (0)1 53 28 19 51
www.damboutons.com

The temple of buttons exists, and is located in Montmartre. At Dam Boutons the buttons, which are sorted by colour, come in every size and shape. Shaped buttons, fancy buttons, in wood or mother of pearl… Here you will definitely find a button that will fire your imagination.

259 LA DROGUERIE

9-11 rue du Jour
A 1 – Louvre &
Les Halles (RB) ③
+33 (0)1 45 08 93 27
www.ladroguerie.com

It seems as if time has stopped here. Disciples of this gorgeous haberdashery shop have been sharing this address with each other for years. The shop itself resembles an old attic with its wood shelves and counters. Here you can find a thousand and one accessories for sewing: buttons, ribbons, tassels, trims, braids… much to the delight of fashion designers and amateur dressmakers alike.

260 ULTRAMOD

3-4 rue de Choiseul
A 2 – Louvre &
Les Halles (RB) ③
+33 (0)1 42 96 98 30

Everything is meticulously arranged in this tiny pretty haberdashery in Sentier, Paris's textile district. The pink and pastel shades add to the girly atmosphere in this store. They organise knitting and sewing courses every Saturday.

257 LA CROIX ET LA MANIÈRE

LES JARDINS DES HÔTELS D'ASSY ET DE BRETEUIL

90 PLACES
TO DISCOVER PARIS

———

The 5 most
EYE-CATCHING
MODERN BUILDINGS

261 IMMEUBLE DE RAPPORT

25bis rue Benjamin-Franklin

A 16

This apartment building, which was built in 1903, is one of the seminal constructions of modernist architecture. With this building Auguste Perret, the architect, demonstrates the new possibilities of a reinforced concrete frame. Here the structure of the façade that has been covered with faience tiles decorated with floral patterns is clearly visible. Part of the façade is recessed allowing for more window space and increasing the light in the rooms of the apartments.

262 L'INSTITUT D'ART ET D'ARCHÉOLOGIE

3 rue Michelet

A 6 – Saint-Germain-des-Prés & Montparnasse (LB) ⑥

In 1928 the architect Paul Bigot designed this building which is a blend of Italian Renaissance and Muslim African influences. The reinforced concrete structure is clad with red bricks from Gournay and an archaeological frieze of terra-cotta moulds of Greco-Roman and medieval sculptures. The building is centred around a large library, surrounded by classrooms.

263 IMMEUBLE À GRADINS

26 rue Vavin
A 6 – Saint-Germain-
des-Prés & Mont-
parnasse (LB) ⑥

In 1912-1913 the architect Henri Sauvage signed the 'manifesto of hygienist architecture'. He invented a stepped structure, which increased the sunlight and ventilation in the apartments, but also allowed him to solve certain hygiene issues and battle tuberculosis. The façade is clad with white ceramic tiles called 'metro', which, as the name indicates, are also used on the walls of the metro stations in Paris.

264 MAISON TZARA

15 avenue Junot
A 18 – Montmartre
(RB) ⑧

In 1926 the architect Adolf Loos went into exile in Paris. During this period he designed a house for his friend, the Dadaist poet Tristan Tzara. The Viennese architect incorporated a cherished principle in this house, his only project in France: simplicity, proof of his commitment to completely strip the façade of a house of all ornaments, in stark contrast with the early 20th century architecture.

265 L'HÔTEL-ATELIER DES FRÈRES MARTEL

10 rue Mallet-Stevens
A 16

In 1927 Robert Mallet-Stevens inaugurated the street named after him, for which he designed all the buildings. The house at number 10 was built for two brothers, the sculptors Joël and Jan Martel. They shared a studio but had separate housing arrangements, which were separated by a staircase to the roof terrace. The architect meanwhile lived at number 12. Unfortunately the design of his home has been somewhat compromised by the two additional floors that were added in the Sixties.

The 5 most striking
CONTEMPORARY
BUILDINGS

---

266 IMMEUBLE MOUCHOTTE

26 rue du
Commandant René
Mouchotte
A 14 – Saint-Germain-
des-Prés & Mont-
parnasse (LB) ⑥

The façade of this building was inspired by the weave of a Scottish fabric. Designed by the architect Jean Dubuisson this building is associated with the Parisian intelligent-sia of the Seventies. It is nicknamed 'the village' because of its active tenants' asso-ciation. Every year in June they organise *la fête Mouchotte* on the ground floor level.

267 FONDATION CARTIER

261 boulevard Raspail
A 14 – Saint-Germain-
des-Prés & Mont-
parnasse (LB) ⑥
fondation.cartier.com

This steel and glass house, designed by Jean Nouvel and inaugurated in 1994, is home to one of the most important privately owned contemporary art foundations in Paris. The building sits in a lush garden. The most remarkable tree in the garden is a Lebanese cedar, which was planted by Chateaubriand in 1825. Above the main entrance is a green wall, which was created in 1998 by the botanist Patrick Blanc.

268 SIÈGE DU PARTI COMMUNISTE

2 place du Colonel
Fabien
A 19 – Belleville &
surroundings (RB) ⑨

This flag-shaped building by the Brazilian architect Oscar Niemeyer dates from 1971. It is a metaphor for a classless society and was deliberately designed to avoid a hierar-chy of spaces. From a structural perspective it is also quite revolutionary. Niemeyer for example worked with Jean Prouvé who designed the glass façade.

269 HÔTEL FOUQUET'S BARRIÈRE

46 avenue Georges V
A 8 – Arc de Triomphe,
Champs-Élysées &
Grands Boulevards
(RB) ②

Edouard François's concept consisted of replicating the authentic Haussman style of the neighbouring building block and using it like a bas-relief on the façades that needed to be renovated. There are large openings in the façade, which are not in any way determined by Haussman's design but which are relevant to the subdivision of the building and the rooms' visual comfort. A hanging garden on the first floor provides an enchanting scenic detail.

270 CITÉ DE LA MODE ET DU DESIGN

34 quai d'Austerlitz
A 13 – Quartier Latin
(LB) ④
www.citemodedesign.fr

These old warehouses, which resemble a concrete barge that has moored for posterity along quai d'Austerlitz, were home to underground Paris in the Eighties. In 2008 the architects Jakob + MacFarlane designed a 'plug-over', changing the building's appearance and shape with a light structure made of etched glass. Nowadays the docks are a popular meeting place, with exhibition spaces, stores, cafés, a club…

The 5 most impressive
TOWER BUILDINGS

271 TOUR ALBERT
33 rue Croulebarbe
A 13 – Quartier Latin
(LB) ④

In 1959 the newspaper *Le Figaro* asked its readers 'Would you like to live on the first floor of the Eiffel Tower?' At the time the first inhabitants were moving into this unique skyscraper in Paris. The sixth floor terrace was decorated with a fresco by Jacques Lagrange, who among others designed the sets for Jacques Tati's films. The building is named after its designer, the architect Edouard Albert.

272 TOUR SUPER-ITALIE
119-121 avenue d'Italie
A 13 – Quartier Latin
(LB) ④

Also known as the round tower this 112-metre high building has been towering over the 13th Arrondissement since 1972. Thanks to the French architect Maurice Novarina the inhabitants have an indoor swimming pool and solarium on the top floor.

273 TOUR FIRST
1-2 place des Saisons
Courbevoie

This tower building, which was designed in 1974, was redesigned from 2007 to 2011, becoming one of the highest buildings in Paris. Since then it is the 'weather girl' of the business district at La Défense. The illumination of the building changes to indicate the next day's weather. Yellow to orange for sun, flickering if it will rain.

274 FLOWER TOWER

23 rue Albert Roussel
A 17

This tower building embodies the desire for nature in the city. The architect Édouard François was inspired by traditional planters and designed a building decorated with giant flower pots with bamboo. The inhabitants are protected from the sun as a result. In order not to excessively burden the balconies the planters were made of fibre-reinforced concrete, a resistant and light material.

275 TOUR TOTEM

57 quai de Grenelle
A 15 – Invalides &
Eiffel Tower (LB) ⑦

This tower building, which was built by the architects Michel Andrault and Pierre Parat, is a residential skyscraper with 207 apartments on 31 floors. Its structure is spectacular. The apartments are situated in the steel and glass cubes that are attached to a visible grid of four columns and 14-metre cantilevered beams.

The most beautiful
BRIDGES

---

276 PASSERELLE SIMONE DE BEAUVOIR

Parc de Bercy
A 13 – Quartier Latin
(LB) ④

The Simone de Beauvoir footbridge was designed by the architect Dietmar Feichtingher and inaugurated in 2006. It connects the forecourt of the François Mitterand library on the left bank with parc de Bercy on the right bank. Its steel structure is composed of two intersecting curves, creating a lens that is also a public space in the middle of the river.

277 PONT NEUF

Rue Dauphine
A 6 – Saint-Germain-
des-Prés & Mont-
parnasse (LB) ⑥

Contrary to its name Pont Neuf (the new bridge) is actually the oldest bridge in Paris. Built in the 16th century this was the first stone bridge that crossed the entire width of the Seine, connecting the left bank, the right bank and the western part of the Île de la Cité with each other. It was also the first bridge without houses. It is however decorated with the first equestrian statue that was ever made, in honour of Henri IV.

278 PASSERELLE DEBILLY

Avenue de New-York
A 8 – Arc de Triomphe,
Champs-Élysées &
Grands Boulevards
(RB) ②

Walk from Palais de Tokyo and the Modern Art Museum of the City of Paris to musée du Quai Branly along this bridge. You wouldn't surmise from its modern appearance and the metal structure that this bridge dates from the World Expo of 1900, for which it was built to ensure visitors could move around freely.

279 PONT SAINT-LOUIS

Rue du Cloître Notre-Dame (Île de la Cité) & rue Jean du Bellay (Île Saint-Louis)
Île de la Cité & Île Saint-Louis ①

Pont Saint-Louis, a simple and modern bridge, connects Île de la Cité to Île Saint-Louis. It is your gateway to the postcard setting that is Paris. Because it is a car-free bridge it is a hassle-free stroll among tourists and artists. From the bridge you can see the apse of Notre-Dame before you enter Île Saint-Louis, a village in the centre of Paris, through rue Saint-Louis en l'île.

280 PASSERELLE DU PARC DES BUTTES CHAUMONT

1 rue Botzaris
A 19 – Belleville & surroundings (RB) ⑨

The suspension bridge of Parc des Buttes Chaumont that was built by Gustave Eiffel allows you to cross the lake 8 metres above ground. If you are not afraid of heights you can enjoy the lake, see the shadows of the fish as they dart through the water and the turtles basking in the sun. The other 22-metre high stone bridge across the lake is called *pont des suicides* and is somewhat concealed by the greenery.

278 PASSERELLE DEBILLY

The five most beautiful
METRO ENTRANCES

281 KIOSQUE DES NOCTAMBULES

Place Colette
A1 – Arc de Triomphe,
Champs-Élysées &
Grands Boulevards
(RB) ②

The entrance to the metro station of Palais Royal-Musée du Louvre, in Place Colette in front of the Comédie Française, was designed by the artist Jean-Michel Othoniel and has become part of the neighbourhood landscape. People use it as a place to meet. The kiosque des Noctambules is easy to recognise because of the aluminium fence around the staircase, which is made of rings with coloured glass inside.

282 CONCORDE

Place de la Concorde
A8 – Arc de Triomphe,
Champs-Élysées &
Grands Boulevards
(RB) ②

Since 1991, the Concorde metro station, on line 12, has been decorated with a ceramic work by the artist Françoise Schein. Read the series of blue letters against a white background and you will realise that you are looking at the full text of the Declaration of Rights of Man and of the Citizen of 1789: you will need to use the vertical blue lines to decipher the 40,000 letters without punctuation.

283 PASSY

Rue de l'Alboni
A16

When travelling on line 6 from Charles de Gaulle-Étoile, when the metro departs in Passy station and travels across pont Bir Hakeim, you have a magnificent view of the Eiffel Tower to your left. On line 5, between Austerlitz and quai de la Rapée, you have a sweeping view of the Cité de la Mode et du Design and its green façade, the National Library, the Panthéon and Centre Pompidou.

284 ARTS ET MÉTIERS

Rue Turbigo
A3 – Marais & Bastille
(RB) ⑤

In the Arts et Métiers station, on line 11, all the furniture, the signs with the name of the station and even the rubbish bins are covered with copper. This was done on the occasion of the bicentenary of the National Conservatory of Arts and Crafts by Benoît Peeters and François Schuiten, the authors of the 'Les Cités Obscures' comic book series. Travellers feel as if they have been immersed in the setting of Twenty Thousands Leagues under the Sea.

285 CLUNY-LA SORBONNE

Boulevard Saint-Michel – Boulevard Saint-Germain
A6 – Quartier Latin
(LB) ④

On line 10, Cluny-La Sorbonne station was decorated in 1988 by the artist Jean Bazaine. The 400 sq.m. mosaic consists of 60,000 glazed lava tiles from Volvic and represents two gigantic birds. The artist also designed the lighting scheme for the station, which is more subdued than in other stations. You can see other works by this artist in Paris at UNESCO and in Maison de la Radio.

281 KIOSQUE DES NOCTAMBULES

The 5 most splendid
LIBRARIES

286 BIBLIOTHÈQUE FORNEY

1 rue du Figuier
A4 – Marais & Bastille
(RB) ⑤
+33 (0)1 42 78 14 60

The Forney Library is the perfect place to work. It is located in the hotel de Sens, one of the few vestiges of civil medieval architecture in Paris and is one of several specialised libraries of the City of Paris. Its collections focus on the decorative arts, on arts and crafts, on fine arts and on the graphic arts. Exhibitions are regularly organised here to highlight the value of the library's collections and promote the arts and crafts.

287 BIBLIOTHÈQUE SAINTE-GENEVIÈVE

10 place du Panthéon
A5 – Quartier Latin
(LB) ④
+33 (0)1 44 41 97 97
www-bsg.univ-paris1.fr

Bibliothèque Sainte-Geneviève is situated alongside the imposing Panthéon in a building that was built in 1851 by the architect Henri Labrouste and which combines stone with cast iron. Any adult with a high school diploma can enter this repository of about two million books. The rectangular reading room is very bright thanks to the forty large windows that run the length of the room.

288 BIBLIOTHÈQUE INHA

2 rue Vivienne
A 2 – Louvre &
Les Halles (RB) ③
+33 (0)1 47 03 89 00

The collections of the library of the INHA or National Institute of History of Art can currently be consulted in the superb 'Oval Room' of the Richelieu quadrangle, which is covered with a magnificent glass dome. Students and art history amateurs can peruse more than one million documents, a digital library, databases and online journals.

289 BIBLIOTHÈQUE MAZARINE

23 quai de Conti
A 6 – Saint-Germain-
des-Prés & Mont-
parnasse (LB) ⑥
+33 (0)1 44 41 44 06
*www.bibliotheque-
mazarine.fr*

Bibliothèque Mazarine is the oldest public library in France having opened in 1643. Its origins lie in the personal collections of Mazarin. Today the library has about 600,000 volumes on the religious, literary and cultural history of the Middle Ages. The library's large gallery, which is definitely worth a look, can be visited for free.

290 BIBLIOTHÈQUE HISTORIQUE DE LA VILLE DE PARIS

24 rue Pavée
A 4 – Marais & Bastille
(RB) ⑤
+33 (0)1 44 59 29 40

The Bibliothèque historique de la ville de Paris or the Historical Library of the City of Paris welcomes all history enthusiasts. Here they can find documents about the city's topographical, political, religious, social and cultural history. The library is in the centre of le Marais in hôtel Renaissance d'Angoulême Lamoignon. The decoration, with crescent moons and the heads of dogs and deer, refer to Diane de France who lived here at one time.

The 5 best places to understand

THE HISTORY
OF PARIS

---

291 PAVILLON DE L'ARSENAL

21 boulevard Morland
A 4 – Marais & Bastille
(RB) ⑤
+33 (0)1 42 76 33 97
www.pavillon-arsenal.com

The Pavillon de l'Arsenal is the perfect place for anyone who loves the architecture of Paris and wants to know more about how it developed over the centuries, what is the state of affairs today and how it is expected to evolve. The pavilion, which dates from 1988, is home to an information and documentation centre, a photo library, a bookshop/store and also organises exhibitions.

292 ROTONDE DE LA VILLETTE

Place de la bataille de Stalingrad
A 10 – Belleville & surroundings (RB) ⑨

The rotunda of La Villette was designed by the architect Claude Nicolas Ledoux between 1784 and 1788. Originally this is where the offices of the *Ferme générale* or customs and excise were located and where you had to pay excise. It survived the plans of baron Haussman, who threatened to demolish it, as well as a fire under La Commune in 1871 and the construction of the metro line 2 which runs around it. Today there is a restaurant, called La Rotonde, here.

293 RÉSERVOIR DE MONTSOURIS

45 avenue Reille
A 14 – Saint-Germain-
des-Prés & Mont-
parnasse (LB) ⑥

Réservoir de Montsouris is the long grass-covered building, with two glass and metal pavilions, along chemin du parc Montsouris, which you can see from the side of the road in rue de la Tombe-Issoire. This masterpiece by the architect Belgrand stores 202,000 m3 of water, which is sourced from Nemours, Provins, Fontainebleau and the Seine Valleys supplying water to 1/5 of the population of Paris.

294 LA RUCHE

21 avenue du Maine
A 14 – Saint-Germain-
des-Prés & Mont-
parnasse (LB) ⑥

La Ruche is not far from Montparnasse and was founded in 1902 by the sculptor Alfred Boucher. This hive-shaped free community arts centre, like Bateau-Lavoir in Montmartre, bears testimony to the artistic profusion in Paris at the time. Today it is still occupied by artists who are following in the illustrious footsteps of artists like Modigliani, Soutine, Brancusi, Léger, Marie Laurencin, and Chagall.

295 LES ARÈNES DE LUTÈCE

47-59 rue Monge
A 5 – Quartier Latin
(LB) ④
+33 (0)1 45 35 02 56

Les arènes de Lutèce, or the arena of Lutetia, which was built in the first century AD, is a Gallo-Roman amphitheatre. It was buried under soil during the construction of the Philippe-Auguste wall in the 14th century but was rediscovered when rue Monge was built. Thanks to the support of Victor Hugo who defended its historical interest it was preserved. Today this is a popular place among people who enjoy a picnic or a game of football.

The five most beautiful
PLACES OF WORSHIP

296 ÉGLISE RUSSE ORTHODOXE SAINT-SERGE DE RADONÈGE

93 rue de Crimée
A 19 – Belleville &
surroundings (RB) ⑨
www.saint-serge.net

At the bottom of Buttes-Chaumont, behind a fence and up a tiny tree-lined path, you will discover a wooden church, similar to the churches you see in Russia. It was built in 1850 for the German workers in the Paris region. Since then it has been frequented by Russian Orthodox church-goers who were driven from their homeland during the 1917 Revolution. A timeless and tranquil place. Visit by appointment or during the Sunday Mass.

297 ÉGLISE SAINT-GERMAIN DE CHARONNE

4 place Saint-Blaise
A 20 – Belleville &
surroundings (RB) ⑨
www.saintgermainde
charonne.fr

You feel as if you are in a village square, with the bakery and the local café on the other side of the street as it should be. The church of Saint-Germain de Charonne is a harmonious combination of remnants from the twelfth, fifteenth and eighteenth centuries. Although you cannot enter the church due to the works (until September 2015) you can continue your walk along the charming garden of the rectory to the cemetery. Saint-German de Charonne is one of the only churches in Paris which still has its old cemetery, a peaceful pastoral location.

298 SYNAGOGUE DE LA RUE PAVÉE

10 rue Pavée
A 3 – Marais & Bastille
(RB) ⑤
+33 (0)1 48 87 21 54

The synagogue in rue Pavée is located in the centre of le Marais. It was designed in 1913 by the architect Hector Guimard for Agudas Hakeholos, a union of Jewish orthodox communities of Russian origin. Nowadays you can only visit it on Heritage Day. Take the time to admire the vertical lines of this façade, which is 12 metres high, a fact that is underscored by the narrow windows and the many pilasters.

299 TEMPLE GANESH

17 rue Pajol
A 18 – Belleville &
surroundings (RB) ⑨
+33 (0)1 40 34 21 89
www.templeganesh.fr

From the outside this looks like a modern building but once inside you are transported to the temples of South India and Asia. Here you can see altars dedicated to Ganesh, Muruga and Shiva, where the faithful leave offerings. There are ceremonies three times a day and a procession for the festival of Ganesh. The temple is also a place of solidarity and has a social function.

300 GRANDE PAGODE DE VINCENNES

40bis route de la
Ceinture du lac
Daumesnil
A 12

The pagoda in bois de Vincennes is the seat of the International Buddhist Institute and the Buddhist Union of France. It is located on the banks of lac Daumesnil in the old pavilion of Cameroon, which was built by the architect Louis-Hippolyte Boileau for the 1931 colonial exhibition. The building was restored in 1977 and transformed into a pagoda for worship. It has the largest Buddha statue in Europe, which is over 9 metres high and is covered with gold leaf.

The 5 most charming
SQUARES

---

301 PLACE GUSTAVE TOUDOUZE

A 9 – Montmartre
(RB) ⑧

This tiny shaded square, with its newspaper kiosk, its Wallace fountain and its restaurants, which is named after the novelist and journalist Gustave Toudouze is popular among the people who live and work in this neighbourhood. Winter or summer the terraces and location of this square make it the perfect place for a breakfast or drinks.

302 PLACE SAINTE-MARTHE

A 10 – Belleville & surroundings (RB) ⑨

This charming square, which has been redesigned in recent years, is only a short walk from the vibrant working-class neighbourhood of Belleville. Gourmet restaurants and groceries opened in the square and the surrounding streets, adding significant value to this building block which has succeeded in retaining its character.

303 PLACE EMILE GOUDEAU

A 18 – Montmartre
(RB) ⑧

The entrance to the new Bateau-Lavoir, which was built in the location of the old centre and which was razed by a fire in 1970, is located in this mythical square in Montmartre. About twenty artists are fortunate enough to have a studio here. The square is also the perfect place for a break after climbing the steep staircases of this neighbourhood.

304 PLACE DAUPHINE

A 6 – Île de la Cité &
Île Saint-Louis ①

This large majestic triangular square, which is hidden between Pont Neuf and the Law Courts, and is lined with restaurants is the perfect place to stop. Watch as people play petanque and lawyers take a break before returning to court.

305 PLACE FURSTENBERG

A 6 – Saint-Germain-des-Prés & Mont-parnasse (LB) ⑥

An iconic square in Saint-Germain-des-Prés. Here you will find all the high-end fabric manufacturers, design shops, galleries and bakeries. Once night falls, when the main light is switched on, this square is transformed into one of the most romantic squares in Paris.

302 PLACE SAINTE-MARTHE

The 5 most
UNEXPECTED VIEWS

―――――

306 **PARC DE BELLEVILLE**

47 rue des Couronnes
A 19 – Belleville &
surroundings (RB) ⑨
+33 (0)1 43 15 20 20

Belleville Park stretches out along the hill of Ménilmontant-Belleville, which is 108 metres high. There is an esplanade at the top which offers sweeping views of Paris. The park was developed in 1988 and has more than 1,200 trees and shrubs, perennials, vines and rose bushes. The landscapers also added some vines, of pinot meunier grapes, in memory of the hill's past as a vineyard. Young children love the playground.

307 **THE ESPLANADE IN FRONT OF THE BASILIQUE DU SACRÉ CŒUR**

35 rue du Chevalier de
la Barre
A 18 – Montmartre
(RB) ⑧
+33 (0)1 53 41 89 00
*www.sacre-coeur-
montmartre.com*

At 130.53 metres this is the highest point of the capital. But the view from Sacré Cœur is probably also the most famous and touristic view of Paris. Here you can see Paris at a glance, especially on clear days with charming Montmartre at your feet, industrial Paris to the east and the Eiffel Tower in the distance. Use the funicular railway, the climb is just as delightful.

308 THE DOME OF PRINTEMPS

64 boulevard
Haussmann
A 9 – Arc de Triomphe,
Champs-Élysées &
Grands Boulevards
(RB) ②
+33 (0)1 42 82 62 76 ??

After shopping at Printemps department store, don't forget to visit the top floor to see the skylight 16 metres above its brasserie, La Coupole. It was built in 1923 after a design of the master glassmaker Brière. The designer Didier Gomez refurbished the brasserie in 2006. His contemporary furniture looks perfect under this magnificent historical monument.

309 THE VIEW OF MONTMARTRE FROM LES BUTTES CHAUMONT

1 rue Botzaris
A 19 – Belleville &
surroundings (RB) ⑨
+33 (0)1 44 52 29 19

If you have the courage and are an athlete then head over to Parc des Buttes Chaumont to climb to the top of this green hill, to the Temple of the Sybil, which was built in 1869 by the architect Gabriel Davioud. You will be rewarded with a splendid view of Montmartre, which lies just in front of you, and Sacré Cœur on the horizon.

310 THE TOP FLOOR OF CENTRE POMPIDOU

Place Georges-
Pompidou
A 4 – Marais & Bastille
(RB) ⑤
+33 (0)1 44 78 12 33
www.centrepompidou.fr

You cannot say that you have visited Centre Pompidou unless you have taken the elevator to the top floor. The terrace of the Le Georges restaurant has the advantage that it is located in the centre of Paris, with an amazing view of the city. We recommend taking the escalators and enjoying the slow ascent, which will give you time to take a closer look at the houses around the Piazza after which you will be finally dazzled by the panoramic view of Paris.

The 5 most
SECRET STREETS

---

311 SQUARE DE MONTSOURIS

8 -12 rue Nansoutis
A 14 – Saint-Germain-des-Prés & Montparnasse (LB) ⑥

This name of this ravishing private road which is lined with individual houses and was built in 1922 refers to nearby Montsouris Park. The most spectacular house is located at the end of the road and was built by Le Corbusier for his friend, the painter Ozenfant. The house with half-timbering that was designed by the architect Gilbert Buisson is also one of the eye-catchers in this street.

312 LA CAMPAGNE À PARIS

Place Octave Chanute
A 20 – Belleville & surroundings (RB) ⑨

The group of streets known as *la campagne* à *Paris* is a building block located on a hill to the east of Paris. The roads are lined with small red brick houses with rose bushes on the façades. They originally were intended as low-income housing given that they were built on the land of an old quarry. Take the staircase to rue Irenée Blanc and explore this idyllic pastoral neighbourhood.

313 RUE CRÉMIEUX

19 rue de Lyon
A 12 – Marais & Bastille (RB) ⑤

Not many tourists and Parisians know that this tiny pedestrian street, which is just a short walk from Gare de Lyon, actually exists. It has 35 free-standing houses with colourful façades. You might be forgiven for thinking you're near Portobello market, with the greens, the yellows, the pinks and the purples.

314 RUE DES THERMOPYLES

32 rue Didot
A 14 – Saint-Germain-
des-Prés & Mont-
parnasse (LB) ⑥

This long narrow cobblestone street, which is lined with private dwellings and workshops, is particularly charming. Stroll through this magical street and you will immediately forget about the hustle and bustle of the city. There are flowers and plants everywhere, the cats roam around freely and lovers walk through this street hand in hand. It also cuts through part of the building block.

315 LA MOUZAÏA

A 19 – Belleville &
surroundings (RB) ⑨

This green enclave near Parc des Buttes Chaumont is like a little island with its tiny houses, flower gardens and steep cobbled streets where it's fun to get lost. Originally this was cheap housing, for working-class people, but nowadays more affluent Parisians live here, in this tiny village in the centre of Paris.

The 5 most

SECRET PASSAGEWAYS

316 COUR DE ROHAN

Rue du Jardinet
A 6 – Saint-Germain-
des-Prés & Mont-
parnasse (LB) ⑥

Cour de Rohan, which is located in La Monnaie neighbourhood in the 6th Arrondissement of Paris, is a veritable oasis of tranquillity, far away from busy boulevard Saint-Germain and carrefour de l'Odéon. You cut through to it through cour du Commerce-Saint-André or rue du Jardinet. In the first of three successive courtyards you can still see the remains of the city wall built by Philippe-Auguste.

317 RUE DU CHAT QUI PÊCHE

9 quai Saint-Michel
A 5 – Quartier Latin
(LB) ④

This secret passage in the Sorbonne neighbourhood runs perpendicular to rue de la Huchette and quai Saint-Michel. It was built in 1540 to give the neighbourhood residents access to the Seine river. Its poetic name probably refers to a fishing tackle shop that used to be here. This is one of the narrowest streets in Paris. At its widest it measures 1.80 metres.

318 RUE BERTON

Avenue de Lamballe /
rue d'Ankara
A 16

Walk down this tiny cobbled alley, which connects rue d'Ankara with avenue de Lamballe and you'll feel as if you've travelled back in time. Midway you will see a milestone that indicates the boundary between Auteuil and Passy. At no. 24 you can still see the green gate through which Honoré de Balzac used to leave the house via rue Raynouard before his creditors arrived.

319 PASSAGE DU GRAND CERF

145 rue Saint-Denis
A 2 – Louvre &
Les Halles (RB) ③

This is one of the best examples of a covered arcade in the neighbourhood. Passage du Grand-Cerf, in the 2nd Arrondissement, takes you from Montorgeuil to Saint-Denis. Its metal and cast iron roof topped with a pretty skylight – the highest in Paris at 12 metres - lets in a lot of light. Here you will find traditional arts and crafts shops as well as furniture and design shops.

320 PASSAGE DAUPHINE

30 Rue Dauphine
A 6 – Saint-Germain-
des-Prés & Mont-
parnasse (LB) ⑥

Passage Dauphine was built in 1825 and connects rue Dauphine with rue Mazarine in the 6th Arrondissement. This private road is located on the site of a former shady club in rue Dauphine, the garden of which extended into rue Mazarine. At no. 20 is a language institute. Its main building is built against a large section of the Philippe-Auguste wall.

319 PASSAGE DU GRAND CERF

316 COUR DE ROHAN

The 5 best
BUS TRIPS

---

321 LE 68

Bus line 68 is a perfect way to get a better idea of how diverse Paris is. It starts in place de Clichy then drives down boulevard de Clichy, passing near Moulin Rouge, past galeries Lafayette, place de l'Opéra and the esplanade of the Louvre. Once past Musée d'Orsay it heads into Saint-Germain-des-Prés. Then it continues along avenue Raspail, where you can spot the famous Le Lutetia hotel.

322 LE 96

Line 96 runs through Paris from south to north. The bus starts from Tour Montparnasse, allowing you to hop off at the magnificent church of Saint-Sulpice. Then you cut through Île de la Cité and arrive at place des Vosges. You then drive past la Maison des Mettalos, the former HQ of the metalworkers' union, which is now a cultural centre. Then it heads to Ménilmontant and finally Porte des Lilas.

323 LE 95

Bus 95 starts at Porte de Vanves, near Parc Georges Brassens. It then drives up to Montparnasse, and then along rue Bonaparte with its many art galleries. Then it continues along pont du Carrousel, offering a splendid view of the Louvre. It continues towards the Opéra, and Saint-Lazare neighbourhood to place de Clichy and finally drives up the hill of Montmartre, stopping at Porte de Montmartre.

324 LE 80

Line 80 leaves from Porte de Versailles, driving along rue de Vaugirard, the longest street in Paris. The bus stops at the Military Academy opposite Champs de Mars and the Eiffel Tower. Once you have crossed Pont de l'Alma you will reach the Champs Élysées, on your left, as the bus drives around the roundabout. Once past Saint-Lazare, the bus continues down rue de Caulaincourt. The terminus is at the town hall of the 18th Arrondissement.

325 THE BOAT BUS

You can visit Paris by boat bus along the river Seine. Your ticket, which is valid for one or two days, allows you to hop on/off at your leisure. The boat stops at the Eiffel Tower, Musée d'Orsay, in Saint-Germain-des-Prés, at the Botanical Garden, the Town Hall, the Louvre and the Champs-Élysées. You can then explore these tourist attractions. Day tickets cost € 16 for adults and € 7 for children.

The 5 most
SECRET GARDENS

---

326 JARDIN CATHERINE LABOURÉ

29 rue de Babylone
A 7 – Invalides &
Eiffel Tower (LB) ⑦

This cottage garden, which is concealed from the street by a high stone wall, is planted with linden trees, poplars, hazelnut trees and vines. Originally it was owned by the community of the Filles de la Charité, whose convent can be seen to the left of the garden. This green pastoral area is the perfect spot for an improvised picnic or some peace and quiet.

327 LES JARDINS DES HÔTELS D'ASSY ET DE BRETEUIL

87 rue Vieille du
Temple
A 3 – Marais & Bastille
(RB) ⑤

In the heart of le Marais you will run into these tiny city gardens, which were in vogue during the Second Empire. They have succeeded in retaining their intimate and romantic atmosphere. It's a place for lovers, teens, the curious and locals to hide, to meet or seek out some peace and quiet. These gardens are enchanting thanks to the mix of rare trees, flowering shrubs and the tiny stream.

328 LE SQUARE DU VERT GALANT

Île de la Cité
A 1 – Île de la Cité & Île
Saint-Louis ①

Located on the western tip of Île de la Cité this tiny square along the Seine affords an exceptional view of the Louvre, hôtel de la Monnaie and Pont Neuf. The tourists that board the *bateaux mouches* do not detract from the splendour of this site. On sunny days the lawns and the area around the garden are invaded by people with picnic baskets.

329 JARDIN ALBERT KAHN

10-14 rue du Port
Boulogne-Billancourt

This Japanese garden pays tribute to Albert Kahn, a renowned nineteenth-century banker, who dedicated his life and fortune to world peace. In memory of his close ties with Japan this unique garden with its wooden bridges, its streams, its banks covered with stones and pink and red azaleas invites you to take a journey to the Land of the Rising Sun.

330 JARDIN SAINT-GILLES GRAND VENEUR

Via le passage du 12
rue Villehardouin & la
petite rue Hesse
A3 – Marais & Bastille
(RB) ⑤

This tiny garden in the middle of a housing block is invisible from the street. But the locals know it well and appreciate the amazing tranquillity of this place. The arbours are covered with climbing roses and there are four lawns with stone benches. It's a perfect place to enjoy your lunch break, let the children run around, read the newspaper or while away the time.

326 JARDIN CATHERINE LABOURÉ

327 LES JARDINS DES HÔTELS D'ASSY ET DE BRETEUIL

5 old
STREET ADVERTISEMENTS
you cannot afford to miss

---

331 BOWLING PUBLICITY
82 rue Mouffetard
A 5 – Quartier Latin
(LB) ④

This slightly flaky painting depicts a couple, in Fifties-style clothes, surrounded by bowling balls and pins. They are looking to the other side of the street. This ad encourages people to cross the street and go to the bowling alley. Don't hesitate to follow the advice and visit this tiny but fun neighbourhood bowling alley.

332 SAVON CADUM PUBLICITY
5 boulevard
Montmartre
A 2 – Louvre &
Les Halles (RB) ③

Take a moment to look up on the busy Grands Boulevards at the advertisement painted here in 1912 by the famous painter and fireman Arsène-Marie, which was recently restored. A baby with blonde curls smiles cutely against a blue background. Subsequently this illustration was used as the brand logo for the well-known French soap brand Cadum.

333 SUZE PUBLICITY
7 rue Barrault
A 13 – Quartier Latin
(LB) ④

On the gable end of a building this ad for liqueur was painted here so you could see it from the street level as well as from the metro viaduct. Nowadays it is partly covered with graffiti and the colours are fading. However it still is a good example of the ubiquitous advertising on the city streets at the time.

334 KUB PUBLICITY

50 rue de Charonne
A11 – Marais & Bastille
(RB) ⑤

This ad for Kub stock is a real masterpiece. It has been very well preserved and covers an entire façade. The artist-upholsterer and designer Christian Zeimert in 1990 added a fun element to this nineteenth-century painted ad, which now reads 'kiss me kub'.

335 CHOCOLATS ROZAN PUBLICITY

1 rue Marx-Dormoy
A18 – Belleville &
surroundings (RB) ⑨

At the time this wall invited people to in-dulge as this ad extolled the benefits of the milk chocolate that was produced in the Pyrenees. It was very successful in the early twentieth century, before it was acquired by the Swiss company Lindt.

332 SAVON CADUM PUBLICITY

The 5 best places to find
STREET ART

336 SPACE INVADER
www.space-invaders.com

This famous street artist has been leaving behind his small mosaic tiles all over Paris for over ten years. These pixellated works are inspired by the famous video game Space Invaders, which was released in 1978. Each 'invader' is unique and perfectly blends in with the city. Look carefully and chances are you might run into a work of this artist, especially in the northeast of Paris.

337 CYKLOP
CITÉ DE L'AMEUBLEMENT:
29 rue de Montreuil –
rue Cesselin
A11 – Marais & Bastille
(RB) ⑤
www.lecyklop.com

This is the pseudonym of Olivier d'Hondt, a visual artist who is working to revitalise street furniture in Paris with his stencil paintings of funny 'Cyklops', whose one colourful eye stares at passers-by. In Cité de l'Ameublement he has transformed the 93 anti-parking bollards of the so-called 'Zoo Street' into zebras, crocodiles, giraffes, leopards and frogs.

338 MISS.TIC
www.missticinparis.com

This feminist artist has been leaving her mark on Paris streets for over thirty years with her silhouettes of *femmes fatales*. She brings walls to life, conveys message, with her stencils and maxims that challenge or disturb you or will even make you smile. This urban poet/artist prefers the streets of the 11th, 13th and 20th Arrondissements.

339 MUR JEFF AÉROSOL
Rue du Cloître Saint-Merri
A4 – Marais & Bastille
(RB) ⑤
www.jefaerosol.com

The famous graffiti artist Jef Aérosol recently completed the gigantic work *CHUUUTTT!!!*, which covers an entire façade near centre Pompidou. A large part of his work is devoted the anonymous people of the street: musicians, passers-by, beggars and children, whose life-size silhouettes he paints, in black and white, always in combination with his signature red arrow.

340 MUR OBEY
Rue Jeanne d'Arc
A13 – Quartier Latin
(LB) ④

At the request of the town hall of the 13th arrondissement the artist Shepard Fairey aka Obey, whose *Hope* portrait of Barack Obama is known the world over, painted a masterpiece on the façade of an apartment building. It is 40 metres high and can be seen from the metro viaduct. The woman holding a huge flower against a bright red background with a black outline adds a certain 'je ne sais quoi' to this rather soulless neighbourhood.

The 5 nicest
WALKS

---

341 LA COULÉE VERTE

Viaduc des Arts
Avenue Daumesnil
A 12 – Marais & Bastille
(RB) ⑤

This green trail runs from Bastille to Porte de Vincennes following the old railway line that used to run here. The 4.5-km long trail uses the railway infrastructure, including the tunnels or bridges. Half of this green corridor runs above the city, about 7 metres above the streets. It is quite an amazing sensation to leave behind the city to walk among the greenery.

342 LA BUTTE AUX CAILLES & LA POTERNE DES PEUPLIERS

Rue des Cinq Diamants
A 13 – Quartier Latin
(LB) ④

Take advantage of a nice sunny day to venture into the streets of la Butte aux Cailles. Stop for lunch at Cailloux, buy some honey at Les abeilles or maybe you prefer an evening walk when the younger crowd flocks to the hill. A little further down you will find La Poterne des Peupliers, a charming block of workers' houses. We recommend stopping at the organic restaurant La bonne heure.

343 PASSAGE BRADY

33 boulevard de
Strasbourg
A 10 – Belleville &
surroundings (RB) ⑨

The atmosphere in Passage Brady, which
is also called Little India, is different. It's
almost like venturing into India. The
owners of the various restaurants try to
attract your attention touting the merits
of their menu. Several shops sell scented
spices and pretty saris. The garlands of
colourful flowers add a festive touch to this
place, which is popular among the locals.
The pinnacle of exoticism.

344 PROMENADE GOURMANDE

A 6 – Saint-Germain-
des-Prés & Mont-
parnasse (LB) ⑥
www.promenadedessens.fr

A good alternative to explore Saint-
Germain-des-Prés through a series of
pleasant encounters. These original
guided visits combine a bit of history of
this mythical neighbourhood with some
tasty stops *en route* in some exclusive
shops including chocolate makers, bakeries
and delicatessens. The ideal way to add some
genuine Parisian addresses to your list.

345 BALADE LE LONG DE LA PETITE CEINTURE

Place Balard
A 15 – Invalides &
Eiffel Tower (LB) ⑦

This railway line, which was built around
Paris under the Second Empire, originally
ran around the capital. Nowadays, a small
section of about one kilometre has been
converted into a walking trail. Although
the railway heritage has been preserved it
has been overrun by nature. Or how to see
Paris from a different perspective…

The sets of 5
CULT FILMS

346 PLACE SAINT-BLAISE
A 20 – Belleville &
surroundings (RB) ⑨

The last scenes of the film *Les tontons flingueurs* by Georges Lautner (1963), with dialogue by Michel Audiard, which starred some amazing French actors like Lino Ventura and Claude Rich, were filmed in and around the church of Saint-Germain-de-Charonne, in place Saint-Blaise, in the 20th Arrondissement. Take a brief pilgrimage to this place and experience the atmosphere of this legendary film.

347 LE TRAIN BLEU
Gare de Lyon
Place Louis Armand
A 12 – Marais & Bastille
(RB) ⑤
+33 (0)1 43 43 09 06
www.le-train-bleu.com

The famous restaurant in Gare du Lyon was used as the backdrop for a major scene in Luc Besson's film *Nikita* in 1990. In it Nikita played by Anne Parillaud receives a birthday gift, a gun which she needs to use to kill a man in the restaurant. The opulent interior only adds to the intensely dramatic scene.

348 DEYROLLE
46 rue du Bac
A 7 – Saint-Germain-des-Prés & Mont-parnasse (LB) ⑥
+33 (0)1 42 22 30 07
www.deyrolle.com

In Woody Allen's film *Midnight in Paris* (2011) Owen Wilson meets Marion Cotillard at Deyrolle for a wedding reception. The famous taxidermy shop, which has become a cabinet of curiosities, is one of the many Paris spots that the director has incorporated in the film.

349 RESTAURANT LA GRANDE CASCADE

Bois de Boulogne
Allée de Longchamp
A 16
+33 (0)1 45 27 33 51
*www.restaurants
parisiens.com*

In *Belle de Jour*, a film by Louis Bunuel (1967), the heroine played by Catherine Deneuve works as a prostitute in the afternoon. She meets one of her 'customers' on the terrace of La Grande Cascade, a restaurant in bois de Boulogne. The elegant setting is perfectly suited to the nature of this discreet encounter with an elegant mysterious man.

350 LES PUCES DE SAINT-OUEN

A 18 – Montmartre
(RB) ⑧

LE DÔME

108 boulevard du
Montparnasse
A 6 – Saint-Germain-
des-Prés & Mont-
parnasse (LB) ⑥
+33 (0)1 43 35 25 81

L'OPÉRA GARNIER

8 rue Scribe
A 9 – Louvre &
Les Halles (RB) ③

Several scenes of *Marathon Man*, a film by John Schlesinger (1976) which stars Dustin Hoffman among others, were filmed in Paris. Some of the sets include the flea market of Saint-Ouen where the rude welcome by the stallholders is slightly exaggerated, the legendary Le Dôme brasserie in Montparnasse and finally the Opéra Garnier and its staircase, which is magnificently filmed.

MUSÉE BOURDELLE

35 PLACES
TO ENJOY CULTURE

The 5 most charming
SMALL MUSEUMS

---

351 MUSÉE DES ARTS FORAINS

53 avenue des Terroirs de France
A 12 – Quartier Latin
(LB) ④
+33 (0)1 43 40 16 22
www.arts-forains.com

The collection of this amazing museum, which is located in a former wine warehouse, consists of millions of rare and dreamlike objects. Here you can see an elephant/hot air balloon, see a unicorn playing the piano and dream away as you look at a belle époque carnival and its wooden merry-go-rounds. This unique place can only be visited by appointment.

352 MUSÉE ZADKINE

100bis rue d'Assas
A 6 – Saint-Germain-des-Prés & Montparnasse (LB) ⑥
+33 (0)1 55 42 77 20
www.zadkine.paris.fr

This small museum, near jardin du Luxembourg, which is set back from the street, was the home and studio of the artist Ossip Zadkine, who lived and worked here from 1928 until 1967. The sculpture garden is a haven of tranquillity and a place to remember this major figure in the École de Paris.

353 MUSÉE DE LA CHASSE ET DE LA NATURE

62 rue des Archives
A 3 – Marais & Bastille
(RB) ⑤
+33 (0)1 53 01 92 40
www.fondation francoissommer.org

This museum, which is located in the historic Marais district, in a 17th- and 18th-century house, resembles a private home. It celebrates animals in painting and the decorative artists. This cabinet of curiosities displays a collection of rare artefacts and contemporary works of art and is certainly worth a visit.

354 GALERIE-MUSÉE DE LA MAISON BACCARAT

11 place des États-Unis
A 16 – Arc de
Triomphe, Champs-
Élysées & Grands
Boulevards (RB) ②
+33 (0)1 40 22 11 00
www.baccarat.fr

The former home of Marie-Laure de Noailles, who used to host the most amazing parties here, is now home to Maison Baccarat. Temporary exhibitions retrace the history of this exceptional crystal manufacturer. Although just a tad kitschy this opulent museum is still very impressive all the same.

355 MUSÉE NISSIM DE CAMONDO

63 rue Monceau
A 8 – Arc de Triomphe,
Champs-Élysées &
Grands Boulevards
(RB) ②
+33 (0)1 53 89 06 40
www.lesartsdecoratifs.fr

This museum, which is located in a private house overlooking parc Monceau, was built by René Sergent in 1912 at the request of Count Nissim de Camondo's only son, Moïse. It is home to a stunning collection of eighteenth-century furniture and artefacts. You visit this magnificent mansion room by room, from the kitchen and the laundry to the reception rooms and the private apartments.

Musée Claude Monet à Giverny
Paris to Vernon train, shuttle bus
from Vernon to Giverny
www.fondation-monet.fr/fr

- Les Arts Decoratifs – connected to
Louvre   www.lesartsdecoratifs.fr

★ Musée Jacquemart-André – audio
tape – Salon de Thé afterwards
158 Blvd Haussman
www.musee-jacquemart-andre.com

185

The 5 most beautiful
ARTIST STUDIOS

---

356 MUSÉE EUGÈNE DELACROIX

6 rue de Furstenberg
A 6 – Saint-Germain-des-Prés & Mont-parnasse (LB) ⑥
+33 (0)1 44 41 86 50
www.musee-delacroix.fr

The Eugène Delacroix museum is in the painter's house and studio and overlooks a delightful private garden. This intimate green oasis in the heart of Saint-Germain-des-Prés is a haven of tranquillity, as the artist originally hoped it would be. The flower beds, which have been reproduced from illustrations, are just as the artist originally wanted and reflect his passion for nature. The benches invite visitors to enjoy the peace and quiet.

357 FONDATION DUBUFFET

137 rue de Sèvres
A 6 – Saint-Germain-des-Prés & Mont-parnasse (LB) ⑥
+33 (0)1 47 34 12 63
www.dubuffet fondation.com

Not many people know about this artist's studio, which nevertheless is one of the most impressive studios in Paris. The artist Jean Dubuffet's immense studio with a skylight is located in a private house at the end of an alley. Nowadays it is a permanent exhibition space, where the works of this painter, sculptor and visual artist and figurehead of the *art brut* movement are exhibited.

358 MUSÉE BOURDELLE

16-18 rue Antoine
Bourdelle
A 15 – Saint-Germain-
des-Prés & Mont-
parnasse (LB) ⑥
+33 (0)1 49 54 73 73
www.bourdelle.paris.fr

This museum/workshop pays tribute to the life and work of the artist Antoine Bourdelle. Time seems to have stood still in this sculpture studio, which is only a short walk from Montparnasse. The stove, the large wooden table and the stools are still here. The atmosphere in this studio is unique and conducive to calm and meditation.

359 APPARTEMENT-ATELIER DE LE CORBUSIER

24 rue Nungesser et
Coli
A 16
+33 (0)1 42 88 75 72
*www.
fondationlecorbusier.fr*

Not many people know about the existence of La Corbusier's apartment and studio. And yet you can visit the master's home every Saturday by appointment. The discovery of this apartment which was entirely designed by the architect and where he lived until his death is both an intimate and an awe-inspiring experience. His favourite furniture and colours, proportions… they are all here.

360 MUSÉE GUSTAVE MOREAU

14 rue de la
Rochefoucauld
A 9 – Montmartre
(RB) ⑧
+33 (0)1 48 74 38 50
www.musee-moreau.fr

The former studio of this symbolist painter occupied the second floor of his family home. Nowadays it is a museum. An impressive staircase connects the large room/studio with the third floor and its two small exhibition spaces. The red walls are covered from floor to ceiling with the artist's paintings, creating a special atmosphere in this museum, that is similar to the one created by Gustave Moreau in the 19th century.

The 5 best

CONTEMPORARY ART GALLERIES

---

361 GALERIE KAMEL MENNOUR

47 rue Saint-André des arts
6 rue du Pont de Lodi
A6 – Saint-Germain-des-Prés & Mont-parnasse (LB) ⑥
+33 (0)1 56 24 03 63
www.kamelmennour.com

This gallery, in the heart of Saint-Germain-des-Prés, in La Vieuville mansion, dates from the 17th century and is owned by the energetic Kamel Mennour. It exhibits work by emerging artists as well as prominent international painters, including Anish Kapoor, Lee Ufan and Daniel Buren who have already had major exhibitions here. The other gallery space, which recently opened, is two blocks away.

362 GALERIE PERROTIN

76 rue de Turenne
A3 – Marais & Bastille (RB) ⑤
+33 (0)1 42 16 79 79
www.perrotin.com

This very trendy gallery has three spaces in le Marais, each more impressive than the other. Although it may feel intimidating to push the door and enter it is definitely worth the detour because here you can see the works of all the leading contemporary artists including Takashi Murakami, Pierre Soulages and Sophie Calle.

363 GALERIE THADDAEUS ROPAC

7 rue Debelleyme
A3 – Marais & Bastille (RB) ⑤
+33 (0)1 42 72 99 00
ropac.net

Another very well-known gallery that represents internationally renowned artist such as Gilbert & George as well as young talent and a few designers. The exaggerated proportions of the gallery's main space makes the exhibitions here very intense.

364 BUGADA & CARGNEL

7 rue de l'Équerre
A 19 – Belleville &
surroundings (RB) ⑨
+33 (0)1 42 71 72 73
www.bugadacargnel.com

This 500 m³ gallery in the east of Paris, established by Claudia Cargnel and Frédéric Bugada, is located in a former garage from the early Thirties. The specialised programme combines exhibits by French and international artists, as well as emerging and established artists.

365 GALERIE MARIAN GOODMAN

79 rue du Temple
A 3 – Marais & Bastille
(RB) ⑤
+33 (0)1 48 04 70 52
*www.marian
goodman.com*

This leading American gallerist who also has galleries in New York and London represents several major contemporary artists including John Baldessari, Tony Cragg and Christian Boltanski and Annette Messager on the French art scene. The exhibitions in the gallery in le Marais can be theoretical and sometimes even disconcerting.

362 GALERIE PERROTIN

The 5 best

GALLERIES FOR ANCIENT ART

---

366 GALERIE CHEVALIER

16 quai Voltaire
A7 – Saint-Germain-
des-Prés & Mont-
parnasse (LB) ⑥
+33 (0)1 42 60 72 68
*www.galerie-
chevalier.com*

Galerie Chevalier is located on Quai Voltaire, in the heart of the prestigious 'Carré Rive Gauche' neighbourhood, where all the antiques dealers can be found. This family-owned business has specialised in antique, modern and contemporary tapestries for four generations. The vestiges of an ancient chapel have been incorporated in this bright space, which is adjacent to the old studio of the painter Jean-Auguste-Dominique Ingres. The tapestries blend in seamlessly in this contemporary setting.

367 GALERIE MALINGUE

26 avenue Matignon
A8 – Arc de Triomphe,
Champs-Élysées &
Grands Boulevards
(RB) ②
+33 (0)1 42 66 60 33
www.malingue.net

For over 30 years Galerie Malingue has been a reference among collectors of masterpieces of the 19th and 20th centuries. The three large exhibition spaces are full of artworks by prominent artists including Cézanne, Picasso, Toulouse-Lautrec, Miró, Dali or Matisse. This place is more than just a gallery, in effect it's a museum.

368 GALERIE STEINITZ

77 rue du Faubourg
Saint-Honoré
A 8 – Arc de Triomphe,
Champs-Élysées &
Grands Boulevards
(RB) ②
+33 (0)1 56 43 66 70
www.steinitz.fr

The world-famous Steinitz Gallery is located in a prestigious mansion along the very chic rue du Faubourg Saint-Honoré. They are recognised worldwide for the rare items they sell and the unparalleled way in which they present them. The period panelling combines beautifully with the artworks, which date from the Middle Ages to the 20th century and which come from Europe, Asia and India.

369 GALERIE KUGEL

25 quai Anatole
France
A 7 – Saint-Germain-
des-Prés & Mont-
parnasse (LB) ⑥
+33 (0)1 42 60 86 23
www.galeriekugel.com

This gallery in Hôtel Collot, on the banks of the river Seine, is one of the most amazing in Paris. Each room has its own specific atmosphere which is perfectly suited to the works of art from different eras that are displayed here. Jewellery, furniture, sculpture, paintings and other precious items are combined in this timeless place. Definitely a must visit for collectors and curators when in Paris.

370 GALERIE GRADIVA

9 quai Voltaire
A 7 – Saint-Germain-
des-Prés & Mont-
parnasse (LB) ⑥
+33 (0)1 42 61 82 06
www.galeriegradiva.com

This prestigious gallery, which is located in a mansion opposite the Louvre, is run by Thomas Bompard, a young art expert specialising in Impressionist and modern art. The majestic staircase, the five successive salons, the library, the African room and dining room serve as the backdrop for a range of eclectic displays that combine works of museum quality, paintings and sculptures as well as manuscripts.

The 5 best

CONTEMPORARY
DESIGN GALLERIES

---

371 CARPENTERS WORKSHOP GALLERY

54 rue de la Verrerie
A4 – Marais & Bastille
(RB) ⑤
+33 (0)1 42 78 80 92
*carpentersworkshop
gallery.com*

Loïc Le Gaillard and Julien Lombrail, the young founders of this gallery, which is ideally located between le Marais and Centre Pompidou, sell furniture that crosses the boundaries of art and design. They like to call it 'utilitarian sculpture'. This large space, on three floors, features the works of internationally renowned contemporary designers to whom the gallery owners give carte blanche.

372 GALERIE KREO

31 rue Dauphine
A6 – Saint-Germain-
des-Prés & Mont-
parnasse (LB) ⑥
+33 (0)1 53 10 23 00
galeriekreo.fr

This laboratory/gallery, dedicated to the research of some of the greatest designers, is managed by Clémence and Didier Krzentowski. Their expertise is world-renowned. They present several exclusive limited edition pieces by such designers as Ronan and Erwan Bouroullec, Konstantin Grcic, Jasper Morrison or Marc Newson. This gallery is considered a reference by collectors and museums.

373 GALERIE GOSSEREZ

3 rue Debelleyme
A3 – Marais & Bastille
(RB) ⑤
+33 (0)6 12 29 90 40
www.galeriegosserez.com

In just a few years this nice gallery in le Marais, which is run by Marie-Bérangère Gosserez, has succeeded in becoming a platform for a new generation of talented designers. Gosserez' unique approach and attention to emerging talent has resulted in a series of exhibitions that do not follow the current fads. Her choices often have proven very wise. The ideal place to start a collection.

374 GALERIE ARMEL SOYER

19-21 rue Chapon
A3 – Marais & Bastille
(RB) ⑤
+33 (0)1 42 55 49 72
www.armelsoyer.com

The gallery in this former leather goods workshop with a courtyard is a new-style gallery. Armel Soyer is passionate about decorative arts, curating works by a handful of contemporary designers whose creative approach pays homage to the great tradition of French workmanship. Although the gallery is mostly visited by decorators and architects do not let this deter you as the visit is definitely worth it.

375 NEXTLEVEL GALERIE

8 rue Charlot
A3 – Marais & Bastille
(RB) ⑤
+33 (0)1 44 54 90 88
www.nextlevelgalerie. com

This vast gallery, which is located in a mansion in le Marais, represents various contemporary artists, designers and photographers. The owner, Isabelle Mesnil, gives free rein to the imagination of these French and international designers. Their works range from conceptual works to utilitarian furniture. She organises six to seven major themed exhibitions and solo shows a year.

The 5 most
CUTTING-EDGE
ARTS CENTRES *in Paris*

---

376 LE LABORATOIRE
4 rue du Bouloi
A 1 – Louvre &
Les Halles (RB) ③
+33 (0)1 78 09 49 50
www.lelaboratoire.org

This centre of experimentation explores the relations between art and science. The researcher, writer and inventor David Edwards came up with this extraordinary concept. The store, which is called LabStore, sells unusual food and environmental innovations, like the now famous 'AeroShot', a small tube of breathable chocolate.

377 LE BAL
6 impasse de la
Défense
A 18 – Montmartre
(RB) ⑧
+33 (0)1 44 70 75 50
www.le-bal.fr

This ballroom, which was built in the Roaring Twenties, has since been converted into one of the most cutting-edge cultural spaces in the city. This independent gallery, which is dedicated to 'the representation of reality by imagery in all its forms', organises exhibitions dedicated to video, cinema, new media or photography. The small bookstore and fun café are also worth visiting.

378 LE LIEU DU DESIGN

11 rue de Cambrai
A19 – Belleville &
surroundings (RB) ⑨
+33 (0)1 40 41 51 02
www.lelieududesign.com

This site wants to build bridges between various people in the design industry, including students, researchers, manufacturers and designers. They regularly organise exhibitions, lectures, meetings and even training sessions here. It is an amazing place of exchanges and experiments in terms of research and innovation.

379 LA GAÎTÉ LYRIQUE

3bis rue Papin
A3 – Marais & Bastille
(RB) ⑤
+33 (0)1 53 01 52 00
gaite-lyrique.net

Visit an exhibition, attend a concert, a lecture or a screening. There is so much you can do at la Gaîté lyrique, a multidisciplinary venue that focuses on digital culture. This meeting space, where you can also have brunch, play video games or obtain information about new technology, is very popular with young hip Parisians.

380 LA MAISON ROUGE

10 boulevard de la
Bastille
A12 – Marais & Bastille
(RB) ⑤
+33 (0)1 40 01 08 81
www.lamaisonrouge.org

This private foundation was established ten years ago on the initiative of the collector Antoine de Galbert who wished to share his passion for contemporary art with the rest of the world. Since then it has become an inspirational place that you really should visit. Solo shows alternate with themed exhibitions. Every year the foundation also presents a major international collection.

ARTISTIC EXCURSIONS
around Paris

---

381 THADDAEUS ROPAC

69 avenue du Général
Leclerc
Pantin
+33 (0)1 55 89 01 10
ropac.net

The gallery owner Thaddaeus Ropac has opened a second exhibition space just a few miles outside of Paris. The renovated 20th-century industrial building has four large light spaces where the gallery organises large-scale exhibitions. It is a magnificent playground for artists. Visitors feel very small when confronted with the outsized art work on display here.

382 GALLERIA CONTINUA

46 rue de la Ferté
Gaucher
Boissy-le-Châtel (Seine-et-Marne)
+33 (0)1 64 20 39 50
*www.galleria
continua.com*

Twice a year this gallery organises stunning contemporary art exhibitions, with monumental works by leading contemporary artists in this old mill and the nearby hangars. And why not take the time to enjoy a picnic on the river bank after your visit?

383 LA GALERIE GAGOSIAN

800 avenue de
l'Europe
Le Bourget
+33 (0)1 48 16 16 47
www.gagosian.com

For this second gallery in France the famous art dealer Larry Gagosian chose an immense space to the north of Paris in the business park at Le Bourget where the private jets land. The architect Jean Nouvel refurbished this Fifties-style building, with a surface area of over 1,650 m³, for the exhibition of monumental sculptures, paintings and installations.

384 LE SILO

**95 route de Bréançon
Marines, Val-d'Oise
+33 (0)1 42 25 22 64**

This magnificent grain silo, which was converted into an art gallery by a couple of minimalist and conceptual art collectors to exhibit their collection there, is open to groups by appointment. (Réservation : lesilo@billarant.com.) The architecture and the works displayed here change every two years and are always very interesting.

385 DOMAINE DE CHAMARANDE

**38 rue du
Commandant Arnoux
Chamarande
+33 (0)1 60 82 52 01**
chamarande.essonne.fr

The Chamarande Estate, a magnificent 98-hectare garden 35 km to the south of Paris, is listed as a 'remarkable garden of France'. Here you can enjoy a picnic, take a bike ride or lie in the sun. But it also has the distinction of being a place that is dedicated to contemporary creation. The garden, the castle and the orangery regularly host fun yet cutting-edge contemporary art exhibitions.

KIDIMO

35 THINGS TO DO WITH CHILDREN

The 5 most
ORIGINAL ACTIVITIES
to do with your children

386 COURS DE YOGA ENFANTS/PARENTS

CHAPS:
3 rue de la Pierre Levée
A 11 – Belleville & surroundings (RB) ⑨
+33 (0)1 43 38 14 52
lasalleparis.com

This yoga and pilates studio offers fun yoga classes which you can take together. Share a moment of complicity and relaxation as well as becoming aware of your body and the space around you. This fun activity for children aged 5 and up and their parents also teaches you to channel your energy.

387 CUEILLETTE EN FAMILLE

Les fermes de Gally
Route de Bailly
Saint-Cyr-l'École
+33 (0)1 30 14 60 60
www.ferme.gally.com

The perfect activity to teach young urbanites about the various seasons and to respect mother Earth. From April onwards this family farm opens its doors to pickers. The children learn to gather fruit and vegetables, strawberries in the summer and pumpkins in the fall, which they can enjoy at home.

388 SÉANCE DE CINÉMA

Cinéma le Balzac
1 rue Balzac
A 8 – Arc de Triomphe, Champs-Élysées & Grands Boulevards (RB) ②
+33 (0)1 45 61 10 60
www.cinemabalzac.com

Once a month, on Sunday mornings, this cinema organises *Pochette surprise* sessions catering to budding film buffs. Young children (age 5 and up) and their parents can discover a selection of short films, which for the most part are silent movies, from the early days of cinema history. A great opportunity to see Charlie Chaplin, Laurel and Hardy, Harold Lloyd and Buster Keaton clown around (again).

(389) LA MAISON DES PETITS

5 rue Curial
A 19 – Belleville &
surroundings (RB) ⑨
+33 (0)1 53 35 50 00
www.104.fr

This intimate and reassuring place was entirely designed with small children in mind, from babies to the age of 5, which is quite rare in Paris. La maison des petits sprung from the mind of Matali Crasset, whose passion for colour and modular approach are widely known. This is where children come to listen, meet other children and create together!

(390) HIPPODROME DE VINCENNES

2 route de la Ferme
A 12
+33 (0)1 49 77 17 17
www.letrot.com

In springtime the Paris-Vincennes hippodrome organises spectacular evening races. From 7 p.m. onwards the temple of trotting becomes a huge open-air stage with spotlights on the race course turning the race into a fascinating and electrifying event. A unique experience, fun for children and what's more, it's affordable too.

Maybe nannies can take them to activities?

The 5 best
TOY STORES

---

391 VILLAGE JOUÉCLUB

5 boulevard des Italiens
A2 – Louvre &
Les Halles (RB) ③
+33 (0)1 53 45 41 41
villageparis.
joueclubdrive.fr

Village JouéClub is located in pretty Passage des Princes. This place is quite unique in Paris as it consists of several toy stores, which is perfect when you have a list of gifts to buy for kids of different ages. There is a wooden toy store, a toy store for toddlers, a playmobil store, a cuddly toy store and even a store that only sells board games and puzzles.

392 LA RÉCRÉATION

36 rue des Bernardins
A5 – Quartier Latin
(LB) ④
+33 (0)1 46 33 88 68

This charming neighbourhood store has been in business for over 35 years. They sell a wide selection of educational and creative toys for children of all ages including some magnificent pedal cars on the pavement outside or hanging from the ceiling. Here the emphasis is on good service, the sales staff takes the time to advise you. Makes a change from the standardised supermarket shelves.

393 CARAVANE FAUBOURG

2 rue Maublanc
A15 – Invalides &
Eiffel Tower (LB) ⑦
+33 (0)1 56 56 55 93
www.caravanefaubourg.fr

This tiny store is chock-full of creative objects and accessories for everyday use: notebooks, schoolbags, satchels, pretty hair pins or funny slippers. Caravane Faubourg is also the perfect place to find all kinds of original gifts for treats at school or for a birthday party: hula hoops, posters that you can colour in or cardboard planes.

394 IL ÉTAIT UNE FOIS

1 rue Cassette
A6 – Saint-Germain-
des-Prés & Mont-
parnasse (LB) ⑥
+33 (0)1 45 48 21 10
www.iletaitunefois-paris.fr

This toy store in Saint-Germain-des-Prés has been here for over 30 years selling a wide array of figurines and amazing costumes for disguising yourself as well as rare and numbered teddy bears, one of a kind items, dolls by artists and old toys. Children and collectors love this enchanting place.

395 VILAC

9 rue de Beaujolais
(Jardins du palais
Royal)
A1 – Louvre &
Les Halles (RB) ③
+33 (0)1 42 60 08 22
www.vilac.com

Since 1911 Vilac has been designing and producing wooden toys for the under fives. In their pretty store near Palais-Royal you will find all sorts of creations including early learning toys, small cars, tricycles, puzzles, stacking and nesting toys. Children and parents alike really love these toys because of the elegant design and the harmonious colours.

The 5 best
COSTUME SHOPS

396 AU CLOWN DE PARIS

160 avenue Ledru-
Rollin
A 12 – Marais & Bastille
(RB) ⑤
+33 (0)1 40 09 74 86
www.auclowndeparis.fr

Despite its large storefront the store itself is tiny. After finding the salesperson, who is hidden behind hundreds of costumes, explore the room that is packed to the hilt with hats, all kinds of gadgets and costumes for adults and children. There is something for everyone: princesses, pirates, fairies, Indians and even mascots. The very friendly owner is happy to help you find what you need.

397 OMY

27 rue Milton
A 9 – Montmartre
(RB) ⑧
+33 (0)1 73 77 22 23
www.omy.fr

This small brand, developed by a graphic designer and an illustrator, sells fun contemporary products, such as clever colouring placemats for when you are dining out as well as paper disguises that can transform you into a pirate or princess. These large paper bags are very easy to slip on: two holes for the arms, one for your head. They fuel children's imagination, as they paint or colour them in.

398 AU FOU RIRE

22bis rue du Faubourg
Montmartre
A9 – Montmartre
(RB) ⑧
+33 (0)1 48 24 75 82
www.aufourire.com

In this festive shop you will find a wide range of accessories including masks, wigs, hairpieces, costume jewellery, all kinds of glasses and even make-up. This tiny boutique is very affordable. And remember, if you can't find it here, you won't find it anywhere.

399 AU COTILLON MODERNE

13 boulevard Voltaire
A11 – Marais & Bastille
(RB) ⑤
+33 (0)1 47 00 43 93
www.cotillonmoderne.fr

Once you cross the threshold of this store you will be struck by the festive atmosphere of this store that sells a wide range of costumes, jokes and tricks. What's special about this store is that they also sell costumes for babies until 12 months. The most unlikely themes are available including cave baby and baby Robin Hood.

400 AUX FEUX DE LA FÊTE

135bis boulevard du
Montparnasse
A6 – Saint-Germain-
des-Prés & Mont-
parnasse (LB) ⑥
+33 (0)1 43 20 60 00
www.auxfeuxdelafete.com

Here you will find all the accessories you need to complete your disguise, including wigs, glasses, hats, red noses and even plastic whistles! This store has all the gadgets you need for your costume parties.

The 5 best parks for a
PICNIC

401 PARC MONTSOURIS

2 rue Gazan
A 14 – Saint-Germain-
des-Prés & Mont-
parnasse (LB) ⑥

This large park to the south of Paris is perfect for a great family day out. Your children won't know where to start first, what with the pony rides, the play areas, the large lawns, the merry-go-rounds and the tunnels they can explore. The ice cream van sells delicious home-made organic sorbets. On weekends it can be busy but you can always find a spot on the lawn for your picnic blanket.

402 LES JARDINS DE BAGATELLE

Route de Sèvres
A 16 (Bois de Bologne)

Considered one of the ten most beautiful parks in the world Bagatelle is also the perfect place for a family picnic. Caves, waterfalls, a rose garden, a small forest or large stretches of grass… it's all there, inviting you to dream away and relax. A nice plus in this historic park is the peacocks that roam around freely, which children always find fascinating.

403 PARC DES BUTTES CHAUMONT

1 rue Botzaris
A 19 – Belleville &
surroundings (RB) ⑨
+33 (0)1 44 52 29 19

This park is one of the largest in Paris so it can be difficult to find your bearings here sometimes. But it is perfectly suited for a walk in the shadows, a picnic at the foot of an old tree or a well-deserved break at the Rosa Bonheur café. Children love hurtling down the large sloping lawns. The late opening hours on Sunday evenings are an added plus.

404 PARC FLORAL DE PARIS

Route de la Pyramide/
Route du Camp de
Manoeuvre
A 12 (Vincennes)
+33 (0)1 49 57 24 84
*www.parcfloral
deparis.com*

Between the castle and the Bois de Vincennes this park is a magnificent foray into nature for children and adults alike. The pine forest, the flower-filled groves, the sweeping lawns and tiny cosy nooks offer plenty of alternatives for a picnic in a magical setting. In spring, when they are planting the borders, many areas are off limits for a family picnic so come during the other seasons.

405 *ZOO* JARDIN DES PLANTES

57 rue Cuvier
A 5 – Quartier Latin
(LB) ④
+33 (0)1 40 79 56 01
www.jardindesplantes.net

nanny ?

This garden is home to the menagerie of the Museum of Natural History of Paris. The zoo opened in 1794, making it the oldest in Paris. There are about 200 different species here, one third endangered. See wild animals, reptiles, monkeys and parrots. Enough to keep your children entertained for hours. Sit down for lunch at one of the picnic tables in the middle of the zoo.

The 5 best places to
HAVE LUNCH
with your kids

---

406 LES 400 COUPS

12bis rue de la Villette
A 19 – Belleville &
surroundings (RB) ⑨
+33 (0)1 40 40 77 78
www.les400coups.eu

This restaurant welcomes parents, children and strollers with a smile. Two mums originally came up with the idea for this unique place. They wanted to develop a friendly space where you could have a hassle-free family lunch. There are changing tables and high chairs on hand, and a play area for your little angels once they have finished gobbling their quinoa. Because the emphasis here is on balanced and tasty seasonal cuisine.

407 LE COMPTOIR GÉNÉRAL

80 quai de Jemmapes
A 10 – Belleville &
surroundings (RB) ⑨
+33 (0)1 44 88 24 48
www.lecomptoir
general.com

This incredible huge warehouse on the banks of canal Saint-Martin is different in that it is part museum, part amusement park. It also has a thrift shop, a bar and a canteen, all in a verdant setting. Its famous weekend brunch is huge fun for children, who run around the various rooms, enjoying the African rhythms. There is even someone on hand to entertain them. We recommend coming early at opening time because the tables and buffets diminish fast.

Weekend Brunch
Go early at Opening

408 LA MANGERIE

7 rue de Jarente
A 4 – Marais & Bastille
(RB) ⑤
+33 (0)1 42 77 49 35
www.la-mangerie.com

If you need a place for a quiet Sunday brunch with your children, then this restaurant in the heart of the Marais has a very attractive proposition. A nanny will take care of your little darlings in a separate room, entertaining them and playing games with them in a party-like atmosphere. Meanwhile, you, the parents can quietly enjoy your delicious brunch. On the way out, your kids receive a small bag of candy treats.

409 MILK

62 rue d'Orsel
A 18 – Montmartre
(RB) ⑧
+33 (0)1 42 59 74 32
www.milk-lepicerie.com

Milk (it stands for 'Mum in her little kitchen') is a gorgeous little canteen where brunch is served every day of the week. The place looks like a vintage diner and is perfect for a mother-daughter lunch. The playful menu is another good reason to go and try out this address.

410 LE CAFÉ DU MUSÉE RODIN

79 rue de Varenne
A 7 – Invalides &
Eiffel Tower (LB) ⑦
+33 (0)1 45 55 84 39
www.musee-rodin.fr

There is a charming café along one of the shady paths in the garden of the Rodin museum. It is the perfect place for a family lunch or a delicious snack. Here the children can run around, play among the sculptures and enjoy the exceptional serenity of this garden in the centre of Paris. The menu includes simple but tasty dishes as well as ice-creams for everyone. The only sour note: you have to pay to get into paradise (2 euros for adults, 1 euro for children).

The 5 most beautiful

DESIGN-FOR-CHILDREN STORES

---

411 KIDIMO

227 rue St-Denis
A 2 – Louvre &
Les Halles (RB) ③
www.kidimo.com

When Nicolas Flachot's daughter was born he found a batch of old letters at the flea market but he only needed three for his daughter's first name. So he started searching for old signs of shops in all sizes, colours and fonts. Now he sells them to professionals and private individuals so they can compose the word or phrase of their choice. You can visit this amazing warehouse by appointment.

412 BALOUGA

1 rue Notre Dame de
Nazareth
A 3 – Marais & Bastille
(RB) ⑤
+33 (0)1 42 74 01 49
www.balouga.com

This shop is the first shop to be fully dedicated to design for children in Paris. They have a wide range of miniature chairs by leading designers such as Harry Bertoia, Arne Jacobsen or Ray and Charles Eames as well as anonymous designs that are more affordable. This place is a must for parents who are collectors as well as parents who want to educate their children about good design from an early age.

413 SERENDIPITY

81 rue du Cherche-Midi
A 6 – Saint-Germain-des-Prés & Mont-parnasse (LB) ⑥
+33 (0)1 42 22 12 18
www.serendipity.fr

This concept store, which is located in an old garage, sells a wide range of vintage furniture and contemporary designs. Although the collection includes all the trendy designers and items you need for to decorate a child's room the store owners have also thought of their parents. Among the cots you can also find tableware, candles and bed linens. They like to combine styles here, so do visit just to take in the decoration scheme.

414 MOMBINI

22 rue Gerbert
A 15 – Invalides & Eiffel Tower (LB) ⑦
+33 (0)1 73 70 62 31
mombini.com

This store is located in a quiet family-friendly neighbourhood, selling all the major popular brands and specialising in Scandinavian brands. Here you can find furniture and decorative items as well as gifts for newborns, or pretty accessories for daily use, like stationery. At the back of the store is a little tearoom with a playroom. Can you think of a better place to end your shopping trip than here, with a tasty snack?

415 LAB.

10 rue Notre-Dame de Lorette
A 9 – Montmartre (RB) ⑧
+33 (0)1 71 39 54 82
www.lab-boutique.com

The young designer of Lab. designed her shop like a tiny cosy apartment. She sells a poetic and flowery range of bed linens and children's accessories, which are all made in France. But she's also thought of the parents, stocking some pretty linen tablecloths in bright colours and a good range of lamps and ceramics.

5 quintessentially
PARISIAN STORES
for children's clothes

---

416 LOUIS LOUISE

83 rue du Cherche
Midi
A6 – Saint-Germain-
des-Prés & Mont-
parnasse (LB) ⑥
+33 (0)9 80 63 85 95
www.louislouise.com

This adorable shop does everything it can
to conquer mum's heart. This neo-bour-
geois, superbly Parisian shop sells ruffled
skirts for little girls, bloomers for babies
and shorts for boys in subtle colours with
delicate prints. Both the summer and
winter collections are always very modern
and poetic.

417 LE MARCHAND D'ÉTOILES

4 rue du Pont aux
Choux
A3 – Marais & Bastille
(RB) ⑤
+33 (0)1 44 78 90 14
www.marchand-
etoiles.com

When the store opened the brand was such
a hit that they have since opened three
more stores in Paris. With a name like that
they must have a lucky star. The concept
is simple yet effective: sprinkle stars on
everything, from jeans pockets to pyjamas.
Children (0-12 yrs) and their parents lap it
up. And what's really nice: the clothes are
affordable too.

418 PETIT PAN

39 rue François Miron
A4 – Marais & Bastille
(RB) ⑤
+33 (0)1 42 74 57 16
www.petitpan.com

With Petit Pan Myriam De Loor wanted
to create a brand dedicated to *joie de vivre*.
Her vision of childhood is multicoloured.
Her creations, which include bed linens,
accessories and clothes sparkle thanks to
the upbeat, bold, punchy, graphic colours.
There are three shops in the same street
so you can explore the designer's different
worlds.

419 FINGER IN THE NOSE

11 rue de l'Échaudé
A6 – Saint-Germain-
des-Prés & Mont-
parnasse (LB) ⑥
+33 (0)9 83 01 76 75
www.fingerinthenose.com

The jeans and down jackets are the best-sellers of this stylish rock 'n roll style kids brand. Finger in the nose clothes above all are functional and durable and a big hit with children and parents alike because they reinterpret current fashion trends.

420 BONTON

5 boulevard des Filles
du Calvaire
A3 – Marais & Bastille
(RB) ⑤
+33 (0)1 42 72 34 69
www.bonton.fr

A favourite haunt among 'Parisian bohos'… although we can easily see why because Bonton is probably one of the prettiest children's clothing shops in Paris. For babies and toddlers. Everything here is simply too pretty to resist, except the prices maybe. You can register your gift list here, a perfect way of avoiding duplicate gifts or errors of taste. As the name suggests, everything here is *bon ton*, or in good taste.

416 LOUIS LOUISE

EDGAR

20 PLACES
TO SLEEP

The 5 best
BOUTIQUE HOTELS

421 HOTEL DES GRANDES ÉCOLES

75 rue du Cardinal
Lemoine
A 5 – Quartier Latin
(LB) ④
+33 (0)1 43 26 79 23
www.hotel-grandes-
ecoles.com

One of the most amazing hotels in Paris is located in the centre of the Quartier Latin, near the Pantheon, at the end of a tree-lined courtyard. And yet it is largely unknown. This beautiful pink town house has 51 rooms with a vintage look and feel. The walls are covered with flowery wallpaper and the rooms furnished with antiques. The highlight is the quiet garden where breakfast is served as soon as the sun rises.

422 HOTEL PARTICULIER MONTMARTRE

23 avenue Junot,
Pavillon D
A 18 – Montmartre
(RB) ⑧
+33 (0)1 53 41 81 40
hotel-particulier-
montmartre.com

This Directoire period home in Montmartre was converted into a boutique hotel a few years ago. The enchanting large private garden makes visitors feel as if they are in large country house instead of in the centre of Paris. The 5 elegant suites were decorated with original themes: contemporary art works are combined with vintage furniture and wallpapers with eye-catching poetic patterns.

423 LE CITIZEN HOTEL

96 quai de Jemmapes
A 10 – Belleville &
surroundings (RB) ⑨
+33 (0)1 83 62 55 50
www.lecitizenhotel.com

Conveniently located on the banks of canal Saint-Martin this three-star hotel has 12 tiny rooms that were decorated by the designer Christophe Delcourt. He used wood throughout the hotel, keeping the design minimalist, fun and bright. The rooms are simple and clean, like ultra-functional cabins, with soft and natural furnishings.

424 HOTEL DU PETIT MOULIN

29-31 rue de Poitou
A 3 – Marais & Bastille
(RB) ⑤
+33 (0)1 42 74 10 10
www.hoteldu
petitmoulin.com

This hotel in the centre of le Marais district is like a wendy house. The designer Christian Lacroix decorated the 16 rooms, creating different, rustic, playful and eccentric worlds in which genres and eras collide to form a quirky yet cosy setting.

425 HOTEL SAINT-THOMAS D'AQUIN

3 rue du Pré aux
Clercs
A 7 – Saint-Germain-
des-Prés & Mont-
parnasse (LB) ⑥
+33 (0)1 42 61 01 22
www.hotel-st-thomas-
daquin.com

Located in a narrow, discreet and charming street in the centre of Saint-Germain-des-Prés, the pretty flower-filled façade of this hotel will immediately catch your eye. The location of this hotel is perfect for visiting the antiques shops and the museums and living life to the rhythm of Paris. The elegant and functional rooms and the quality of the service will only enhance your stay.

The 5
HIPPEST HOTELS

---

426 **HOTEL PARADIS**

41 rue des Petites-
Écuries
A 10 – Belleville &
surroundings (RB) ⑨
+33 (0)1 45 23 08 22
www.hotelparadisparis.
com

This tiny hotel has 10 rooms and was decorated by the young fashionable decorator
Dorothée Meilichzon. She has succeeded in
creating an intimate and inspiring atmosphere by combining Scandinavian furniture
with bold wallpaper and industrial details.
The reading area, which gives out onto the
street and the breakfast room, invite you
to hang around and read a book like you
would at home.

427 **EDGAR**

31 rue d'Alexandrie
A 2 – Louvre &
Les Halles (RB) ③
+33 (0)1 40 41 05 19
www.edgarparis.com

This owner wanted this hotel, which is
located in the centre of Quartier du Sentier
with its many textile shops, to feel like
a family home. So he asked his friends,
his cousin and even his father in law (the
famous photographer Yann Artus Bertrand)
to decorate the 13 rooms to add character
and soul. Lunch in the restaurant and
terrace which give out onto a tiny shady
square is simply delightful.

428 HOTEL HENRIETTE

9 rue des Gobelins
A 13 – Saint-Germain-
des-Prés & Mont-
parnasse (LB) ⑥
+33 (0)1 47 07 26 90
www.hotelhenriette.com

This small hotel, which has only 32 rooms, is located on a small cobbled street near the Latin Quarter, and the perfect place for an inspiring stop in Paris. You will feel right at home in this intimate, feminine place where the delicate combination of old furniture, soothing colours and design is bound to appeal to anyone who loves beautiful interiors that are designed with great care.

429 HOTEL AMOUR

8 rue Navarin
A 9 – Montmartre
(RB) ⑧
+33 (0)1 48 78 31 80
www.hotelamourparis.fr

Since this hotel opened all of the Paris in crowd has spent the night or a few hours here because this old rendez-vous hotel also rents rooms from 12 noon to 3 p.m. The decoration scheme is love and eroticism in a superbly Parisian way: all the rooms contain work by contemporary artists and graphic designers in combination with vintage furniture and artefacts. There is an outdoor garden with lush vegetation where you can immerse yourself in the festive ambiance.

430 THOUMIEUX

79 rue Saint-
Dominique
A 7 – Invalides &
Eiffel Tower (LB) ⑦
+33 (0)1 47 05 49 75
www.thoumieux.fr

This luxury hotel is located above brasserie Thoumieux and has 12 rooms. It was decorated by India Mahdavi, who worked close-ly with the owner, Chef Jean-François Piège. The feminine, voluptuous and colourful style of this decorator works perfectly with the intimate brasserie and its impeccable service. If you are looking for a chic and discreet place to sleep in Paris, this is it.

The 5 best hotels for

A ROOM WITH AN IMPRESSIVE VIEW

431 HOTEL RAPHAEL

17 avenue Kléber
A 1 – Arc de Triomphe,
Champs-Élysées &
Grands Boulevards
(RB) ②
+33 (0)1 53 64 32 00
www.raphael-hotel.com

Enter this very chic five-star hotel, which is only a short walk from the Arc de Triomphe, walk directly to the elevators and head to the top floor. There you will find a hanging garden with an amazing view over the rooftops of Paris. On sunny days you can enjoy breakfast on this terrace, a dizzying and unique quiet oasis.

432 SHANGRI-LA HOTEL

10 avenue d'Iéna
A 16 – Arc de
Triomphe, Champs-
Élysées & Grands
Boulevards (RB) ②
+33 (0)1 53 67 19 98
www.shangri-la.com

This five-star hotel in the former home of Prince Roland Bonaparte is all about its exceptional location. Although the majority of the rooms have unbeatable views some, like the Shangri-La and the Chaillot Suite, can rely on the Eiffel Tower for a guest appearance. The summer terrace, which is open to everybody, is a unique yet discreet place where you can enjoy a delicious cocktail while admiring the sunset.

433 GRAND HOTEL DU PALAIS-ROYAL

4 rue de Valois
A 1 – Louvre &
Les Halles (RB) ③
+33 (0)1 42 96 15 35
www.grandhoteldupalais
royal.com

Pierre-Yves Rochon, the star decorator of palaces, refurbished this five-star hotel. He has spared no effort to make it look just as sumptuous as the nearby Palais Royal as well as highlighting the different views from this ideally located hotel. You can enjoy the stunning architecture of Paris to the full in the majority of the rooms, whether they give out onto the State Council or the Ministry of Culture or have a view of Paris and its monuments.

434 LE CINQ CODET

5 rue Louis Codet
A7 – Invalides & Eiffel
Tower (LB) ⑦
+33 (0)1 53 85 15 60
www.le5codet.com

This atypical hotel between the Eiffel tower and Les Invalides is perfect when you're looking for the peace and calm of the 7th arrondissement. This intimate place to stay, located in a historic industrial building from the Thirties and decorated by Jean-Philippe Nuel, has four suites with a view. The upscale 'Dôme' suite comes with a breathtaking view of the city and a Jacuzzi on the terrace, while guests in the junior suites can enjoy the view of the three-hundred-year-old dome of Les Invalides from their bathtub – not too bad either.

435 LE BRISTOL

112 rue du Faubourg
Saint-Honoré
A 8 – Arc de Triomphe,
Champs-Élysées &
Grands Boulevards
(RB) ②
+33 (0)1 53 43 43 00
www.lebristolparis.com

This Parisian palace has 4 suites that are decorated in full-blown 18th-century style. Every one of them boasts a wonderful view. The *Suite Panoramique* has a flower-filled terrace that overlooks the capital. The *Lune de Miel* or Honeymoon Suite is even more spectacular, offering a stunning view of the most beautiful monuments in the city. If you decide to book a 'standard room' know that the swimming pool and terrace with solarium on the sixth floor come with an equally magnificent view of Paris.

The 5 most
MYTHICAL HOTELS

436 L'HOTEL

13 rue des Beaux Arts
A 6 – Saint-Germain-
des-Prés & Mont-
parnasse (LB) ⑥
+33 (0)1 44 41 99 00
www.l-hotel.com

This intimate hotel is one of the mythical hotels in Saint-Germain-des-Prés. Its impressive spiral staircase, the baroque and at times even downright theatrical decoration of the rooms, the private pool under the arches and the bar, a meeting place where artists, actors and Parisian personalities contributed to the legend of this hotel where Oscar Wilde lived in 1898.

437 REGINA

2 place des Pyramides
A 1 – Arc de Triomphe,
Champs-Élysées &
Grands Boulevards
(RB) ②
+33 (0)1 42 60 31 10
www.regina-hotel.com

This upscale establishment opened in 1900 for the World Expo. The family that owned it had been working in the hospitality for several generations. Its Art Nouveau interior, a symbol of French luxury, was used as a backdrop for many a film. The Regina faces the Louvre Museum and the Tuileries Gardens. All the fashionistas stay here during Fashion Week.

438 LE BEL AMI

7-11 rue Saint-Benoît
A 6 – Saint-Germain-
des-Prés & Mont-
parnasse (LB) ⑥
+33 (0)1 42 61 53 53
www.hotelbelami-
paris.com

This hotel is named after the eponymous well-known masterpiece of nineteenth-century French literature by Guy de Maupassant. It is one of the landmarks of Saint-Germain-des-Prés, like Café Flore, Les Deux Magots and Brasserie Lipp which is just a short walk from the hotel. The recently renovated hotel's contemporary style embodies the intellectual and bourgeois French spirit.

439 LE PAVILLON DE LA REINE

28 place des Vosges
A 3 – Marais & Bastille
(RB) ⑤
+33 (0)1 40 29 19 19
www.pavillon-de-la-reine.
com

Set back slightly from place des Vosges this hotel is named after Anne of Austria who stayed here. It is perfectly suited to guests who prefer peace and quiet, discreet luxury as well as the lively and genuine spirit of Paris. This four-star hotel has 54 rooms and suites. Its beautiful ivy-covered façade and sheltered garden allow you to participate in neighbourhood life, for example as you walk past children on their way to school.

440 HOTEL DU NORD

102 quai de Jemmapes
A 10 – Belleville &
surroundings (RB) ⑨
+33 (0)1 40 40 78 78
www.hoteldunord.org

In 1938 Hôtel du Nord, along canal Saint-Martin, acquired legendary status thanks to the film that Marcel Carné made here. Although you can no longer rent a room here it is still a mythical hotel in the minds of many movie fans and Parisians. It reopened 10 years ago as a pleasant bar-restaurant with a crowd of regulars and tourists.

LE SILENCIO

35 PLACES
TO GO OUT

The 5 best
CONCERT HALLS

---

441 LA MAROQUINERIE

23 rue Boyer
A 20 – Belleville &
surroundings (RB) ⑨
+33 (0)1 40 33 35 05
www.lamaroquinerie.fr

This iconic venue has always championed an eclectic programme, which is dominated by international rock. Since its opening in 1997 La Maroquinerie is the place of choice for this musical aesthetic. The restaurant-bar regularly hosts lectures, debates and exhibitions, turning it into a real art space.

442 LE TRIANON

80 boulevard de
Rochechouart
A 18 – Montmartre
(RB) ⑧
+33 (0)1 44 92 78 00
www.letrianon.fr

Le Trianon has been fully restored with respect for the history of this place, its ballroom and winter garden and its theatre with balconies. Today it is one the most beautiful concert halls in Paris. The varied programme includes classical concerts by the Symphonic Orchestra of Europe, French chansons and renowned international artists.

443 LES TROIS BAUDETS

64 boulevard de Clichy
A 18 – Montmartre
(RB) ⑧
+33 (0)1 42 62 33 33
www.lestroisbaudets.com

Les Trois Baudets is a mythical concert hall in Pigalle. In the Fifties several renowned artists were discovered here, like Brassens, Brel and even Gainsbourg. Nowadays Les Trois Baudets continues to serve as a springboard for a generation of French artists. The concert hall also has a restaurant with a panoramic view of boulevard de Clichy, making it the preferred meeting place for music professionals who are looking to discover emerging artists.

444 LA MAISON DE LA RADIO

116 avenue du
Président Kennedy
A 16 – Invalides &
Eiffel Tower (LB) ⑦
+33 (0)1 56 40 22 22
maison.radiofrance.fr

La Maison de la Radio was inaugurated in 1963. The building was designed by the architect Henry Bernard for the French public broadcaster. As a result the centre over the years has hosted several free concerts in its magnificent studios, ranging from classical to contemporary music.

445 LA LOGE

77 rue de Charonne
A 11 – Marais & Bastille
(RB) ⑤
+33 (0)1 40 09 70 40
www.lalogeparis.fr

La Loge is a tiny concert hall, only a short walk from place de la Bastille. This former recording studio has perfect sound and acoustics, making it the perfect venue for light and original concerts that were specially developed for it. La Loge is located in a beautiful private listed courtyard, making this family-friendly place even more charming.

The 5 most
BEUTIFUL THEATRES

---

446 LA CARTOUCHERIE

Route du Champ de
Manœuvre
A 12
+33 (0)1 43 74 24 08
www.cartoucherie.fr

La Cartoucherie, which is located in bois
de Vincennes, consists of several theatres
including Théâtre de la Tempête, Théâtre
de l'Aquarium and Théâtre du Soleil. It was
founded in the Seventies and nowadays
is managed by Ariane Mnouchkine. This
former arms factory is a green oasis, and
an idyllic place to take in a performance or
simply enjoy a break.

447 THÉÂTRE DES BOUFFES DU NORD

37bis boulevard de la
Chapelle
A 10 – Belleville &
surroundings (RB) ⑨
+33 (0)1 46 07 34 50
www.bouffesdunord.com

Les Bouffes du Nord undoubtedly is the
most beautiful theatre in Paris. For many
years it has been associated with Peter
Brook who staged several productions here,
which are considered iconic performances
in theatre history. In recent seasons the
programming has given pride of place
to contemporary productions and young
theatre companies.

448 LE DANSOIR

Bibliothèque
Nationale de France
11 quai François
Mauriac
A 13
+33 (0)1 48 05 46 22
ledansoir.saporta-
danse.com

Le Dansoir is a dance theatre that pops up in different locations around the city. The circular theatre is in fact a magic mirror tent, made of solid oak and fitted with mirrors and red velvet drapes. The atmosphere is quite intimate here as the audience is close to the stage. At Le Dansoir you can see the choreographies of the centre's director Karine Saporta among others.

449 THÉÂTRE DE L'ODÉON

Place de l'Odéon
A 6 – Saint-Germain-
des-Prés & Mont-
parnasse (LB) ⑥
+33 (0)1 44 85 40 40
www.theatre-odeon.eu

The Théâtre National de l'Odéon is a French theatrical institution, playing a very important role in Parisian cultural life since its establishment in 1782. The Doric order and the austerity of the cubic elements of the façade distinguish this historical building in the 6th Arrondissement from others. In recent years another theatre, called 'Les Ateliers Berthier', in boulevard des Maréchaux, has also opened. All the leading actors in French theatre have performed here.

450 THÉÂTRE DE L'ATELIER

1 place Charles Dullin
A 18 – Montmartre
(RB) ⑧
+33 (0)1 46 06 49 24
www.theatre-atelier.com

L'Atelier is a beautiful Italian-style theatre in a charming square in Montmartre. The programme mainly includes stagings of plays by renowned playwrights like Becket, Duras and Pinter. Stars of the cinema and theatre regularly perform here.

The 5 best
FESTIVALS

451 ROCK EN SEINE

Parc de Saint-Cloud
Domaine national de
Saint-Cloud
Saint-Cloud
www.rockenseine.com

Attracting over 100,000 people every year during the last weekend of August Rock en Seine is the perfect festival to mark the end of the summer. Major international rock bands and smaller emerging bands perform on different stages in a magnificent French-style garden in an electrifying atmosphere.

452 VILLETTE SONIQUE

Parc de la Villette
211 avenue Jean-Jaurès
www.villettesonique.com

The programme of Villette Sonique Festival, which is organised in various venues in the east of Paris, like Cabaret Sauvage, Trabendo and Cité de la musique, is a mix of electronic music, rock and hip-hop. Various free open-air concerts are also organised in parc de la Villette (end of May – early June – the dates change from year to year).

453 WE LOVE GREEN

Parc de Bagatelle
42 route de Sèvres à
Neuilly
A 16
www.welovegreen.fr

In the heart of the magnificent parc de Bagatelle this environment-friendly festival is mainly geared towards pop, indie rock and folk fans. The perfect event to enjoy music, being outdoors, organic locally sourced food and take part in debates about sustainable development and responsible artistic creation. The last weekend of May.

454 MO'FO

Main d'œuvres
1 rue Charles Garnier
Saint-Ouen
www.festivalmofo.org

This independent music festival is organised with just one thing in mind: discovering new bands. In the midwinter MO'FO warms your body and soul in a beautiful venue, Main d'oeuvres. The emphasis is on indie bands, without focussing on a specific music format. A small festival which prefers a more human scale and a close relationship with the artists. The last weekend of January.

455 LES FEMMES S'EN MÊLENT

www.lfsm.net

Since 2001 this festival has celebrated the independent female performance scene, which is becoming increasingly free and different. Originally it started out as one concert to celebrate Women's Day. Nowadays the event is organised over several weeks in March in various venues in Paris and all over France. This festival pays tribute to female artists, whether international or emerging.

The 5 most
UNEXPECTED PLACES TO HAVE FUN

---

456 CHINATOWN OLYMPIADES

44 avenue d'Ivry
A13 – Saint-Germain-
des-Prés & Mont-
parnasse (LB) ⑥
+33 (0)1 45 84 72 21
*www.chinatown
olympiades.com*

Chinatown Olympiades is the place for you if you like an exotic taste and cultural experience. After having enjoyed some dumplings and Peking duck, it's time for some music and karaoke. The songs keep on coming in every possible language from English to French, Khmer and Chinese of course. The atmosphere is amazing.

457 LA GUINGUETTE CHEZ GÉGÈNE

162bis allée des
Guinguettes
Quai de Polangis
Joinville-le-pont
+33 (0)1 48 83 29 43
www.chez-gegene.fr

This mythical *guinguette*, which is open from April to mid-December, and which has been photographed by some of the greatest photographers like Robert Dois-neau, is the perfect place to capture the spirit of the early twentieth century and party on the banks of the Marne. Here they regularly organise dinner dances and theme nights. The ambiance is genuine and unique.

458 LE MOONSHINER

5 rue Sedaine
A11 – Marais & Bastille
(RB) ⑤
+33 (0)9 50 73 12 99

At first glance this place may look like a simple neighbourhood pizzeria. But 'Da Vito' is actually a front for a clandestine cocktail bar with an amazing atmosphere. The Moonshiner is an original place to meet friends or surprise someone on a first date. Go to this unusual restaurant and bar for an original evening on the town.

459 PETIT BAIN

7 port de la Gare
A 13
+33 (0)1 80 48 49 81
www.petitbain.org

This pretty floating barge with amazing views of the river Seine is a restaurant, bar and concert hall. This unusual 'floating cultural facility' is where you go to hear some Vietnamese rock or Turkish tango, while sipping cocktails on the verdant terrace.

460 LE CARMEN

34 rue Duperré
A 9 – Montmartre
(RB) ⑧
+33 (0)1 45 26 50 00
www.le-carmen.fr

This mansion used to be a brothel but was converted into a private club. The spectacular boudoir-style scenery attracts a young and trendy crowd which enjoys the mix of DJ sets and acoustic concerts. The contrast between the venue and the people who frequent it is rather striking.

460 LE CARMEN

The 5 best clubs to
PARTY AFTER
MIDNIGHT

---

461 LE SILENCIO
142 rue Montmartre
A 2 – Louvre &
Les Halles (RB) ③
silencio-club.com

The interior design and furniture of this private club was designed by David Lynch. This gem in the depths of the capital consists of several spaces (a concert hall, a mini cinema, an art library, bars, smoking room) which you get to after walking down six dim flights of stairs. Claustrophobes may probably find this difficult but once you're in the club the atmosphere is amazing.

462 YOYO
Palais de Tokyo
13 avenue du
Président Wilson
A 16 – Arc de
Triomphe, Champs-
Élysées & Grands
Boulevards (RB) ②
+33 (0)1 81 97 35 88
yoyo-paris.com
www.palaisdetokyo.com

This underground club in the cellars of the experimental arts centre Palais de Tokyo is popular among electronic music lovers. This bare concrete space which is lit by video projects is where the young contemporary scene performs. The atmosphere here is very uninhibited.

463 BATOFAR

FACING:

11 quai François
Mauriac
A 13 – Quartier Latin
(LB) ④
+33 (0)1 53 60 17 00
www.batofar.org

This boat which is moored on the Seine is a must of Paris nightlife. With its metal cabin that has been painted red and its tall lighthouse you can see it from afar. The naval architecture and the electronic music are the hallmarks of this unusual club. In the summertime the boat's pleasant terraces are also ideally suited for cocktails in the evening.

464 LA BOÎTE À FRISSONS

13 rue au Maire
A 3 – Marais & Bastille
(RB) ⑤
+33 (0)1 42 72 17 78
www.boite-a-frissons.fr

In this Fifties-style club the atmosphere is friendly and relaxed. La Boîte à Frissons is located in the heart of le Marais and is popular with gays, lesbians, and straight people alike. Here you always dance with someone, whether to rock 'n roll, a waltz or a tango until half past midnight. Then everyone breaks into a line dance after which it's time for some disco music.

465 NÜBA

36 quai d'Austerlitz
A 13 – Quartier Latin
(LB) ④
+33 (0)1 76 77 34 85
www.nuba-paris.fr

This club overlooks the Seine from the roof terrace of the Cité de la Mode et du Design. The summery and casual atmosphere is appreciated by fans of the electro sets by famous DJs. As soon as the summer hits this hanging garden becomes the place to see and be seen.

5 places for a
NIGHT-TIME SNACK

466 AU PIED DE COCHON

6 rue Coquillière
A1 – Louvre &
Les Halles (RB) ③
+33 (0)1 40 13 77 00
www.pieddecochon.com

This mythical brasserie in Quartier des Halles is open 24/7. Although they serve every possible pork dish the grilled trotter is the house's speciality, which the more adventurous are bound to enjoy. Night owls enjoy the old-style Paris restaurant and its friendly atmosphere.

467 LE TAMBOUR

41 rue Montmartre
A2 – Louvre &
Les Halles (RB) ③
+33 (0)1 42 33 06 90

Here you can enjoy traditional French cuisine until 3.30 a.m. People go there for the decoration scheme, made of old metro maps and bus stops that have been recycled as chairs, the animated conversations between the owner and the regulars rather than for the cooking which is not really that refined. This is a true neighbourhood institution, where you can meet all kinds of funny types at night.

468 LA MAISON DE L'AUBRAC

37 rue Marbeuf
A8 – Arc de Triomphe,
Champs-Élysées &
Grands Boulevards
(RB) ②
+33 (0)1 43 59 05 14
www.maison-aubrac.com

This Auvergnat restaurant, which is only a short walk from the Champs-Élysées and is renowned for the quality of its meat and its excellent wine list, is open day and night. The beef they serve here, which they source from their own family farm in Aubrac, is the perfect choice after a long meeting or a night out clubbing.

469 LA POULE AU POT

9 rue Vauvilliers
A1 – Louvre &
Les Halles (RB) ③
+33 (0)1 42 36 32 96
www.lapouleaupot.com

This elegant restaurant with its authentic Thirties-style decoration serves braised chicken, an iconic and traditional French dish, until 5 a.m. in the morning. The restaurant opened in 1935 and has earned a solid reputation among night owls. Legend has it that many stars end the night here.

470 AU GÉNÉRAL LAFAYETTE

52 rue la Fayette
A9 – Arc de Triomphe,
Champs-Élysées &
Grands Boulevards
(RB) ②
+33 (0)1 47 70 59 08
www.au-general-lafayette.com

This beautiful timeless brasserie serves good regional cuisine every day until 3 a.m. At the end of the evening all the artists and actors who work in the nearby theatres tend to flock here.

The 5 most
BEAUTIFUL CINEMAS

471 LOUXOR

170 boulevard
Magenta
A 10 – Belleville &
surroundings (RB) ⑨
+33 (0)1 44 63 96 96
www.cinemalouxor.fr

The architect Henri Zipcy designed this stunning historical venue in 1921. It recently regained some of its lustre after a thorough restoration. The large cinema, which is nicknamed 'la Pharaonne' with its golden scarabs, cobras and balconies immerses cinema goers into an exotic world. The Louxor's bar, with its terrace that gives out onto Sacré-Coeur and boulevard Barbes is perfect for an after-movie drink.

472 LE CHAMPOLLION

51 rue des Écoles
A 5 – Quartier Latin
(LB) ④
+33 (0)1 43 54 51 60
www.lechampo.com

This arthouse cinema which Parisians know and love opened in 1938. Nowadays it is listed as a historical monument. Every month they organise 'Les nuits du Champo' from midnight onwards. The package includes three films and breakfast. This cinema also regularly organises major retrospectives.

473 NOUVEL ODÉON

6 rue de l'École de
Médecine
A 6 – Saint-Germain-
des-Prés & Mont-
parnasse (LB) ⑥
+33 (0)1 46 33 43 71
www.nouvelodeon.com

Matali Crasset designed this arthouse cinema as a friendly, colourful and outgoing space. Every three months they organise exceptional evenings, film previews and meetings with actors here.

474 PAGODE

57bis rue de Babylone
A 7 – Invalides &
Eiffel Tower (LB) ⑦
+33 (0)1 45 55 48 48
*www.etoile-cinemas.com/
pagode/*

This cinema is located in a pagoda that was built in 1896 by the architect Alexandre Marcel. It is one of the most unusual and exotic places in Paris, especially because of its Japanese cinema. The charming garden, which is listed as a historical monument, is a nice place to have a drink after the film.

475 CINÉMA EN PLEIN AIR

211 avenue Jean Jaurès
A 19 – Belleville &
surroundings (RB) ⑨
+33 (0)1 40 03 75 75
www.villette.com

Every summer parc de la Villette is converted into a temporary cinema, showing timeless classics as well as unknown feature films. Films which you watch as night falls, sitting on the grass after a picnic with friends. The film is free, you only have to pay for your lawn chair.

472 LE CHAMPO

LA COUPOLE DU PRINTEMPS

25 RANDOM GOOD-TO-KNOW PLACES AND URBAN DETAILS

5 houses of
FAMOUS PEOPLE

---

476 LA MAISON DE BALZAC

47 rue Raynouard
A 16 – ⑦
+33 (0)1 55 74 41 80

Nowadays the house where the writer Honoré de Balzac lived for 7 years, in the heart of the village of Passy, is a museum. You can step into his study where he wrote some of his masterpieces like *La Cousine Bette* or *Une ténébreuse affaire*. The writer particularly appreciated the quiet cool garden, which is an excellent hideaway on hot summer days.

477 LA MAISON DE VICTOR HUGO

6 place des Vosges
A 4 – Marais & Bastille
(RB) ⑤
+33 (0)1 42 72 10 16
*www.maisonsvictorhugo.
paris.fr*

If you happen to pass through the prestigious place des Vosges, then visit the apartment where Victor Hugo and his family lived for 16 years. Nowadays it is a museum, but the many documents and testimonials recreate the atmosphere of the place when the writer lived here. Immerse yourself in the private world of this famous French intellectual as you admire the furniture, artefacts and artworks that belonged to him.

478 LA MAISON DE DALIDA

11bis rue d'Orchampt
A 18 – Montmartre
(RB) ⑧

Perched on the hill of Montmartre at the end of an alley near the famous Moulin de la Galette this mansion from 1900 was where this star lived from 1962 until her death in 1987. She chose this quiet oasis far from the bustling city to enjoy the space and a bit of freedom. Her impressive grave is nearby in the cemetery of Montmartre.

479 LA MAISON DE SERGE GAINSBOURG

5bis rue de Verneuil
A 7 – Saint-Germain-
des-Prés & Mont-
parnasse (LB) ⑥

The Parisians know this house very well as it would be hard to overlook this house in a very chic street in the 7th Arrondissement where the famous singer-songwriter lived for over twenty years. The mythical façade, which is covered with drawings, graffiti and admiring messages left by fans has become a place of contemplation. There was some talk about turning this sanctuary into a museum but the project remains on hold.

480 LA MAISON DE GEORGES BRASSENS

7 impasse Florimont
A 14 – Saint-Germain-
des-Prés & Mont-
parnasse (LB) ⑥

The French poet-author-composer and singer lived in this house at the end of an adorable no-through road with colourful houses from 1944 until 1966. Here he wrote his first songs like *Le Gorille* and *Margot*. He remained loyal to this house, even after he became famous.

The 5 best
WEBSITES
about Paris

---

481 **CHOCOLATE & ZUCCHINI**
chocolateandzucchini.com

Clotilde Dusoulier, who is passionate about cooking, started her culinary blog about 10 years ago. This Parisian bloggers scours Paris for the best restaurants, bars, grocery stores, markets and so on, sharing this info with her readers. She also posts recipes, recommends books and products. Her expertise and the success of her blog are such that Clotilde is now a journalist, author and consultant.

482 **MY LITTLE PARIS**
www.mylittleparis.com

Every day this website posts new ideas for outings, unusual walks, good restaurants, places where you can have a secret rendez-vous, or do something different. A young, intrepid and well informed team unearths all these tips. Among others, you can find the address of a chignon bar, a place where you can rent sunglasses and even a restaurant where you can dine by yourself on this website.

483 MERCI ALFRED
www.mercialfred.com

Alfred scours Paris on his moped in search of the best places to go in Paris: trendy bars, the restaurants where truckers go or forgotten institutions. But Alfred is also a true gentleman who advises young urban men to live better in Paris with (life)style and sport tips.

484 QUE FAIRE À PARIS ?
quefaire.paris.fr

This site is your guide for all outings, with a spirit of resourcefulness, humour and authenticity. They post various themed smart articles every week, like 'What to do in Paris with your grandmother?' *Que faire à Paris?* is an online magazine, which has all the best tips for cultural trips, outings and activities at affordable prices.

485 LES BALADES DE MAGALIE
www.lesbalades demagalie.com

Magalie has three passions: Paris, art and travel. Walking is a way of life for her which is why she develops some inspired itineraries. One of them is *l'Heure bleue du soir*: when the sun has set but night has not quite fallen yet and Paris becomes a city of light, with a range of unique colours. The walks devised by Magali are poetic and dreamy. (Walks also available in English.)

The 5 best
PLACES TO WORK
for freelancers

---

486 ARTICHAUT-COWORKING

16 boulevard Saint-Denis
A 10 – Belleville & surroundings (RB) ⑨
+33 (0)1 71 20 22 13
artichaut-coworking.com

When the architect Julie Alazard became self-employed she was unable to find the perfect office. So she set up a co-working space instead buying up old offices which she tastefully redesigned, converting them into a contemporary and soothing space. There are eighteen workstations here in this 150 m3-space, which you can rent by the week or by the month. You can also use the meeting room if you book it on the schedule first.

487 CRAFT

24 rue des Vinaigriers
A 10 – Belleville & surroundings (RB) ⑨
+33 (0)1 40 35 90 77
cafe-craft.com

Craft is a café for independent designers. It was designed so they could work in comfortable and optimal conditions: there are sockets so you can plug in your laptop, a fast Wi-Fi connection, Ethernet plugs and more. The nice black and white decoration scheme was dreamt up by two young designers which go by the name of Pool. The cappuccino is delicious and you can spend the day here. The headquarters of all the freelancers in this neighbourhood.

488 ANTICAFÉ

79 rue Quincampoix
A3 – Marais & Bastille
(RB) ⑤
+33 (0)1 73 73 10 74
anticafe.fr

Here you pay for the time you spend here. 4 euros an hour or 14 euros for the entire day. The rate includes the café and snacks as well as free Wi-Fi access, a scanner, a printer, a projector, the library and the game library. The ideal place to work in a quiet setting or exchange ideas with the people at the neighbouring table in a thought-provoking environment.

489 LA CHAMBRE AUX OISEAUX

48 rue Bichat
A10 – Belleville &
surroundings (RB) ⑨
+33 (0)1 40 18 98 49
lachambreauxoiseaux.
tumblr.com

This nice café, which has been decorated to look like a country house with mismatched furniture and flowery wallpaper, welcomes people and their laptops. Here you will run into bloggers or groups of girls who enjoy coming here for a tasty pastry. You can sit here all day, the Wi-Fi is at your disposal and the ambiance is generally very peaceful.

490 LES ATELIERS DRAFT

12 esplanade Nathalie
Sarraute
A18 – Montmartre
(RB) ⑧
+33 (0)9 81 01 02 17
www.ateliers-draft.com

Looking for a workplace for 3 hours or 3 months? For a studio that comes with tools like a fretsaw, a sewing machine or a 3D printer? Or are you perhaps looking for a meeting spot where you can share and discuss ideas with likeminded people? Les Ateliers Draft are a one-of-a-kind co-working space for independent creatives. Here they can work out a project from the beginning to the end in an arty and stimulating atmosphere.

The 5 best places to
PRACTICE SPORT

---

491 ÉLÉPHANT PANAME
10 rue Volney
A 2 – Arc de Triomphe,
Champs-Élysées &
Grands Boulevards
(RB) ②
+33 (0)1 49 27 83 33
*www.elephant
paname.com*

The Éléphant Paname cultural centre is located in a nice mansion that was built under Napoleon III. This is a multidisciplinary and friendly place, which is ran by two siblings, Fanny and Laurent Fiat, a dancer and a visual artist. They regularly schedule nice exhibitions here but you can also follow a dance course. Classical, jazz, oriental, hip hop, capoeira… there is something for everyone, regardless of your level.

492 RUNNING TOUR
*www.parisrunningtour.
com*

If you like to explore Paris from a different perspective then why not combine a cultural itinerary with some jogging? Run along the banks of the Seine past some stunning Parisian monuments, under the iconic bridges of Paris, through deserted squares and enjoy the morning light while Paris wakes up. That is what www.parisrunningtour.com promises.

493 LES TERRAINS DE TENNIS DU JARDIN DU LUXEMBOURG
3 rue Guynemer
A 6 – Saint-Germain-
des-Prés & Mont-
parnasse (LB) ⑥
+33 (0)1 43 25 79 18

This place is a favourite with Parisians who like to practice sports. As a result you need to book one of the six tennis courts of the Jardins du Luxembourg well in advance in order to have a free slot. But what a pleasure and privilege to play tennis in one of the most beautiful historic gardens in the city!

494 PISCINE DE PONTOISE

19 rue de Pontoise
A5 – Quartier Latin
(LB) ④
+33 (0)1 55 42 77 88

This listed red brick building, which was designed in 1934 by the architect Lucien Pollet, is home to one of the most beautiful swimming pools in the capital. The 33-metre pool has a magnificent glass roof and Art Deco-style individual changing cabins. Fitness fans will be happy to know it also has gym facilities, including cardio equipment, a weight room and a sauna. The pool is known for its late opening hours and cleanliness.

495 LE BATTLING CLUB

13 rue de la Grange aux Belles
A10 – Belleville & surroundings (RB) ⑨
+33 (0)1 42 01 24 12
www.battlingclub.com

This former warehouse which has been converted into a tiny gym for men, women and children, offers combat sports classes: English and French boxing, wrestling or free fighting. The regulars like the fact that it is nearby canal Saint-Martin so they can enjoy a drink on the terrace after their workout.

491 ÉLÉPHANT PANAME

5 events that determine
THE LIFE OF PARISIANS

496 SALON EMMAÜS
PARIS EXPO
PORTE DE VERSAILLES:
1 place de la Porte de
Versailles
A 15
www.emmaus-france.org

The Emmaüs association has been a pioneer of sustainable development for over 60 years, organising a great sale for international solidarity once a year. All recycling enthusiasts, inveterate bargain hunters and anyone who likes a good deal flock here to shop among an incredible selection of thousands of clothing items, furniture, bikes, books, vinyl records, toys and many others useful items.

497 FIAC
GRAND PALAIS:
Avenue Winston
Churchill
A 8 – Arc de Triomphe,
Champs-Élysées &
Grands Boulevards
(RB) ②
www.fiac.com

The international contemporary art fair which is held under the magnificent skylight of the Grand Palais is the social and artistic event of the year. More than one hundred galleries from around the world display works by well-known and emerging artists. Events and exhibitions are organised on this occasion for the whole city, which focuses on nothing else but contemporary art for the duration of the fair.

498 SALON DE L'AGRICULTURE

PARIS EXPO
PORTE DE VERSAILLES:
1 place de la Porte de
Versailles
A 15
*www.salon-agriculture.
com*

This event is the most important agricultural fair in France, attracting thousands of visitors. For one week 1,300 exhibitors from 22 countries gather here. This is an exceptional opportunity to showcase regional products and regional and international cuisine. At the same time you can also see hundreds of animals here, who have left their meadows and barns for an excursion to Paris.

499 RETROMOBILE

PARIS EXPO
PORTE DE VERSAILLES:
1 place de la Porte de
Versailles
A 15
www.retromobile.com

The Retromobile fair is the annual event for anyone who collects or loves vintage cars. Hundreds of cars and motorcycles are exhibited here every year in February. The fair is estimated to attract about 90,000 visitors. This event is also a wonderful opportunity to meet with car professionals, like restorers, body shops and spare parts dealers.

500 LE MARATHON DE PARIS

*schneiderelectric
parismarathon.com*

The marathon of Paris is one of the five biggest running events worldwide. This legendary race over a course of 42.195 km has been organised every year since 1976. It's a great opportunity for athletes to invade the city, from Champs-Élysées to bois de Vincennes, as they run along avenue Foch and are cheered on by the crowd.

INDEX

COLOPHON

The 500 Hidden Secrets of Paris
Marie Farman

ENGLISH TRANSLATION — Sandy Logan
GRAPHIC DESIGN — Joke Gossé and Tinne Luyten
PHOTOGRAPHY – Joram Van Holen and Tino van den Berg

The addresses in this book have been selected after thorough independent research by the authors, in collaboration with Luster Publishers. The selection is solely based on personal evaluation of the business by the authors. Nothing in this book was published in exchange for payment or benefits of any kind.

D/2014/12.005/14

ISBN 978 94 6058 1373

NUR 506

© 2014, Luster, Antwerp
Third updated edition, August 2015
www.lusterweb.com
info@lusterweb.com

Printed in Belgium (Bruges) by Die Keure.